DISCLAIMER

Dr. Melissa Caudle, On the Lot Productions, LLC, nor Open Door Publishing House cannot guaruntee that by following the information in this book your screenplay, or film, will get green light or be accepted by television networks or production studios as a result of writing your synopsis.

This book was written for educational purposes only and not as legal, tax, or accounting advice. We cannot be responsible for any document or synopsis you create as a result of this book. We cannot take any responsibility with what the reader does with the informaiton we provide and any documents the reader produces should be reviewed by a qualified entertainment attorney in the state in which you live. Each state has unique laws.

Likewise, only an attorney can give legal advice and only an accountant can give financial advice. When dealing with the entertainment industry, always seek professional advice. Likewise, always register your completed work, film, screenplays, treatments, synopis, and loglines with either the Writer's Guild of America or the U.S. Library of Congress.

On the Lot Productions, LLC nor Dr. Melissa Caudle accepts unsolicted scripts, screenplays, business plans, or reality show projects. For information on how to submit your project visit www.onthelotproductions.com.

Register for a free newsletter at www.therealityofrealitytv.com for the latest information on screenwriting and creating reality shows by Dr. Melissa Caudle.

BOOKS IN THE SCREENWRITING GUIDEBOOK SERIES

ALL BOOKS AVAILABLE ON AMAZON.COM, BARNES & NOBLE, AND BOOKS A MILLION

HOW TO WRITE A SYNOPSIS
Quick Guidebook for Screenwriters

DR. MELISSA CAUDLE

PUBLISHER

www.opendoorpublishers.com
Publisher since 2005

www.onthelotproductions.com

 is registered trademarks of On the Lot Productions, LLC (Logo created by Melanie Bledsoe)

ISBN-13: 978-1468084870
ISBN-10: 1468084879

Cover and interior designs: Dr. Melissa Caudle
Copy proof editor: Robby Cook Stroud
Cover filmstrip photograph credits: Photography Credits in the Appendix

Graphic logos and designs: On the Lot Productions, LLC and are Copyright Protected

Author Picture by Tim Moree
Introduction montage design: On the Lot Productions, LLC – Individual Photo Credits Listed in the Appendix
Chapter 1 montage design: On the Lot Productions, LLC – Individual Photo Credits Listed in the Appendix
Chapter 2 photo: Post Card created by On the Lot Productions, LLC – Bloody Photo by Simon Howden
Chapter 3 photo: Hoda Hahn and Dr. Mel Caudle
Chapter 4 photo: JZ Creationz
Chapter 5 photo: Roland Darby
Chapter 6 photo: Salvatore Vuono
Chapter 7 photo: On the Lot Productions, LLC
Chapter 8 photo: On the Lot Productions, LLC
Chapter 9 photo: Hoda Hahn, Salvatore Vuono, and Idea Go
Chapter 10 photo: Salvatore Vuono, Hoda Hahn, and Raymond Rizzoto
Chapter 11 photo: Hoda Hahn, Salvatore Vuono, and Exdos
Chapter 12 photo: Salvatore Vuono
Chapter 13 photo: Hoda Hahn, Idea Go, Salvatore Vuono, and Putt Sky
Chapter 14 photo: Simon Howden
Chapter 15 photo: Dr. Mel Caudle
Chapter 16 photo: Steven Valenci and Simon Howden
Chapter 17 photo: montage design by On the Lot Productions, LLC
Chapter 18 photo: Kong Sky
Chapter 19 photo: Hoda Hahn, Putt Sky, Salvatore Vuono

HOW TO WRITE SYNOPSIS

Quick Guidebook for Screenwriters

By

Dr. Melissa Caudle

www.opendoorpublishinghouse.com

TABLE OF CONTENTS

ACKNOWLEDGEMENT

Screenwriter Roger Corman, American film producer, director and actor, said,

> *"You can make a movie about anything as long as it has a hook to hang the advertising on."*

I say,

> *"Life is stranger than fiction and any movie or reality show should be about life and those who live it."*

I have to acknowledge the people in my life that have made it a wonderful life and interesting to live. There never seems to be a dull moment as a wife, mother, mother-in-law, grandmother, littlest, sister, aunt, producer, reality show creator, director, screenwriter, author, mentor, and friend. Those special and dear to my heart know who you are. My life is what it is because your lives touched mine.

"Who needs a fantasy when I have my reality?" **Dr. Melissa Caudle**

DEDICATION

MY PARENTS
William W. and Helen V. Ray

MY HUSBAND
Michael Caudle

MY CHILDREN AND THEIR FAMILIES
Erin and Dimitris and sons Stamatis and Elias
Kelly and Roger Jr. and son Roger III
Jamie and Haunnard and to my future grandchildren

MY SIBLINGS
Denny, Livia, Caylen, and Robby

MY PEERS
Vicky Thomas, Mark Freehelm, Kevin Williamson, Piers Anthony, Dr. Felisa Wolfe-Simon, Beau Marks, Stephen Esteb, Robert Downey Jr., Shamar Moore, J.P. Prieto, Darren Sharper, Ron Lurie, James Woods, Kate Bosworth, James Marsden, Alexander Skarsgaurd, Drew Powell, Rhys Corio, Billy Lush, Dominic Purcell, Marc Friedman, Arlena Acree, Vince Vance, Brett Butler, Fran Drescher, Carmen Electra, Josh Gad, Anne Rice, Neema Barnette, Nina Henderson-Moore, Gina Holland, Jamie Balthazar, Dallas Montgomery, Jodie Jones, Andy Sparaco, David C. Kirtland, Tracy Davenport, Duane Gross, Michael Ragsdale, Jimmy Fallon, David Replogle, Salvatore Vuono, Dr. Carol Michaels, Nicolas Cage, The Swider Brothers, Ronald D. Moore, Sir Anthony Hopkins, Michael Heisman, Kevin Costner, Kenneth Johnson, Jamie Fox, Gordon Peck Jr., Kelly Marcel, Derrick Berry, Laz Alonzo, Ernie Banks, Jeff Galpin, Ted Lange, Governor Buddy Roemer, Jaqueline Flemming, Suzie Labry, Bill Donavan, Lenni Kravitz, Rhys Coiro, Billy Lush, Anson Mount, Walton Goggins, Carmen Electra, Susy Labry, Michael Mann, Wayne Morgan, Steven Zaillian, Peter Frampton, Justin Beiber, Brittney Spears, Derrick Barry, Jimmy Kimbell, Ray Bradbury, Jim Morrison, Charlie Daniels, Janet Leahy, Glenn Gainor, Patrick Stewart, Geraldo Rivero, Phil Donahue, Senn Penn, Hisako Matsui, Emily Mortimer, Martin Lawrence, Nathan Scott, Joe Montegna, Stevie Nicks, John Lands, Jude Law, Stehpen Rue, Lance Nichols, The Olsen Twins, Blain Kern, Robyn Batherson, Lucy Lawless, Mike Anderson, John Andeson, Liz Coulon, Ryan Glorioso, Jim Morrison, Nancy Grace, George Flynn, Ray Fields, James Mance Jr., Sara Gruen, Ann Gibbs, Patrick Taylor, Sean Penn, Jonathan

Frakes, Morena Baccarin, Kelly Preston, Connie Chung, Mel Gibson, Melissa Leo, Ken Follett, Criss Angel, Mathieu Kassovitz, Dominic Purcell, Stevie Nicks, Melissa Leo, Ally Sheedy, Gary Grubbs, Kendra Wilkinson, Anne Massey, Holly Madison, David Hebert, John Sayles, Bridget Marquardt, Graham Nelson, Beau Bridges, Melissa Peterman, Raymond Chandler, Elizebeth George, Lou Angeli, Jeffery Roberson (AKA Varla Jean Merman), Mark Cortale, Ryan Dufrene, Dusty Wilson, Nick Phillips, Judd Nelson, Hugh Hefner, Michael Crawford, Radha Mitchell, Bill Klein, Jennifer Arnold, Benjamin Hurvitz, Eli Holzman, Amanda Stutevoss Coppola, Sheldon Lazarus, Jude Law, Jay Leno, Simon Cowell, Ellen DeGeneres, Paula Abdul, Morgan Freeman, L.L. Cool Jay, Queen Latiffa, Nina Garcia, Eminem, Pamela Anderson, Dorian Dardar, Adam Lambert, Andrew Gurland, Veronica Kelly, Kevin Costner, Adam Horowitz, Wendy Smith, Kelsy Grammer, Chris Koffer, Dean Develin, Michelle Nicolette Kowalski, Callie Moore, Wendie Malick, Lacey Chabert, Mark Haddon, Sylvester Stallone, Steve Purcell, Jim Jarmusch, Lou Angelie, Joe Hausterhaus, Janice Engel, Connie Chung, Former Governor Buddy Roemer, Suzanne Pleshett, Delta Burke, Rob Marshall, Isaac Bashevis Singer, Marie Scott, Thomas Moore, Lucy Lawless, Timohy Robbins, Jimmy Buffett, Jimmy Kimmel, James Franco, Simon Howden, Ken Follett, Jeff Davis, Jessica Simpson, Erica Messer, Ed Bernero, Jonathan Carroll, J.P. Perez, Simon Mirren, Foster Remington, Johnny Knoxville, Seann William Scott, Burt Reynolds, Willie Nelson, Lynda Carter, Tom Selleck, Ernie Banks, Eric Paulson, Sally Ann Roberts, Hoda Kotb, Vidal Sassoon, Debra Fisher, Andrew Wilder and Magan Laren, Wayne Morgan, Lance Moore, Reggie Bush, Evan Lysacek, Billy Ray Hobley, Tracy Portier, Chris Ivory, Drew Brees, Roman Harper, Christopher Gray, Marin Lawrence, Cuba Gooding Jr., Mary Tyler Moore, Scott Moran, Phebe Hurst Middleton, Don Knotts, Sally Ann Robertson, Patrick Evans, Johnny Weir, Parker Armstrong, Nathaniel Baker, T.D. Jakes, Dr. James Meza, Shiri Appleby, Eyal Podell, Zach and Shantell Nasits, Ashton Phillips, Michael Douglas, Ellen DeGeneres, John Goodman, Malcom Petal, Mark Burnett, Tim Hightower, Tracy Miller, Martha Stewart, Donny Osmond, John Dupre, Madame Elisandrya De Sade, Govenor Bobby Jindal, Senator Gary Hart, Jonathan Rhys Meyers, Randy Quaid, Penny Marshall, Enya, Haley Reinhart, James Durban, Tom Cantwell, Diablo Cody, Brad Pitt, Nicholas Cage, John Landis, Tim Owens, Matt Damon and his mother Nancy Carlsson-Paige, Steven Seagal, Jason Priestley, and Trevor Jones

MY BESTFRIENDS WHO ARE MY PETS
To my Chihuhuas Gizmo and Lola,
To my African Albino Dwraf Frogs Fric III and Frac

SPECIAL THANKS

TO THOSE THAT HAVE ALWAYS BELIEVED IN ME, INSPIRED ME, AND HELPED MAKE MY DREAMS TO COME TRUE. YOU KNOW WHO YOU ARE.

TO ROBBY COOK STROUD, FOR HER PROOF EDITING. IT MEANS THE WORLD TO ME.

TO JAMIE ALYSON, FEATURED THROUGHOUT THIS BOOK, AS BLAZE, IN THE SCREENPLAY *THE KEYSTROKE KILLER*, MAY ALL YOUR DREAMS COME TRUE. ONE DAY, I WANT THAT INVITATION TO THE ACADEMY AWARDS WHEN YOU RECEIVE BEST ACTRESS.

Jamie Alyson and Dr. Mel on the way to a wrap party after filming.

INTRODUCTION

WHAT'S UP WITH THAT?

"Normally I work out a general summary of what I mean to do, then start writing, and the details can be different from my anticipation. So there is considerable flow, but always within channels." **Piers Anthony – Science Fiction Writer best known for the series *Xanth***

THE BRAIN FREEZE

Do you shiver at the thought of having to write a synopsis or sweat bullets as if the thermostat on your heater is set at 120-degree? Do you experience brain-freeze? Don't feel that you are alone. In fact, most screenwriters feel this same way. Somehow, it is easier to write a 125-page screenplay than to narrow it to three to four paragraphs that fits a single page. Why? Because, condensing pages isn't easy. It is a challenge for screenwriters because they are prolific at writing and enjoy the power of words.

We get into a mind-set that more is better. However, when you write a synopsis, less is better. Choose your words carefully and every word count. There isn't room for fluff. That is why it is so mind boggling to write a synopsis and it's not easy. If it were, I wouldn't have written this book and you wouldn't have purchased it. There wouldn't be any need.

I hope that after you read this book, your anxiety of writing a synopsis decreases and your thermostat is brought down. Believe me; at first, it wasn't easy for me either. Somehow, I can sit down and write a 300-page book with no fear or hesitation. Whatever I am thinking easily transfers to the written page. I average writing 15 pages each day. Yet, when I sit and write a synopsis for one of my screenplays, it can take me all day just to write the first draft. Once, it took me three days. My husband was in shock. He couldn't believe that it took me three days to write one page when he witnesses me write 50 – 60 pages in that amount of time. He accused me of having writer's block.

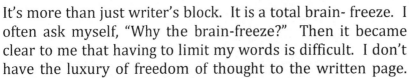

It's more than just writer's block. It is a total brain- freeze. I often ask myself, "Why the brain-freeze?" Then it became clear to me that having to limit my words is difficult. I don't have the luxury of freedom of thought to the written page. That's when I devised a plan to use every time I must write a synopsis. By following my own formula, my brain-freeze melts. This formula is what I present in this book.

PRACTICE MAKES PERFECT

You often hear that practice makes perfect. I don't agree. I say, "Perfect practice makes perfect." You can practice wrong all day long and never get it right. That is why it is important to learn the basics of a synopsis long before you start to write one.

There are two ways you learn to write a perfect synopsis, trial and error, or application through learning. Personally, learning to write a synopsis through trial and error isn't the way to go. First, you don't know if you are getting it right or wrong. Second, it takes numerous attempts with many countless hours that you could spend elsewhere. Finally, you often come away more frustrated.

Learning through application is a better way to learn because the information you learn is acquired and mastered. Skill and knowledge doesn't occur randomly or through happenstance. Rather, knowledge acquired through guidance and demonstration is more effective. The time you spend in a guided learning situation is less than the time learning through trial and error.

REALLY! WHAT IS UP WITH THAT?

How to Write a Synopsis: Quick Reference Guide for Screenwriters provides a powerful tool in writing a synopsis for a screenplay. A synopsis is important in many ways:

- Provides a summary of your screenplay.
- Allows a manager, agent, or producer to become acquainted with your screenplay.
- Provides focus to the screenwriter when writing a screenplay.
- Used as one of many marketing tools for your screenplay.

This book is part of a book series written especially for screenwriters.

The other books in this series are:

- *How to Write a Logline: Quick Guidebook for Screenwriters*
- *How to Create a One Pager: Quick Guidebook for Screenwriters*
- *Writing Loglines, Synopsis, and a One Pager for Film and Reality TV*

Although written last in this series, *Just Beat it! Quick Guidebook for Screenwriters* is now available after numerous requests by first-time screenwriters. This book, takes the screenwriter on the journey to create a design a beat sheet for a short film, a

feature-length film, and a one-hour episodic television pilot program. Most importantly, several Beat Sheet Evaluation forms and Beat Sheet Development Forms designed by the author are included in this book. I use these forms every time I write a screenplay or one of the episodes for *The Keystroke Killer*. If you plan to submit a spec script for *The Keystroke Killer* television series, using the beat sheet provided in this book will prove beneficial in your quest for your episode to fit within the parameters established by the development department. Use this form every time when developing a screenplay. It really helps.

Coming soon are additional books including *How to Develop a Short Film into a Television Series.* This book discusses how I developed the short film script into a television series. Included in this book is not only the short film script, but also the first pilot episode script Transcendence. It will take you behind the scenes as I created the television series. How often do you get that opportunity?

THE KEYSTROKE KILLER

I wrote the screenplay, *The Keystroke Killer,* to use in all quick guidebooks in this series as a learning tool. I want everyone to begin with the same reference point to learn each topic presented in the quick guidebooks.

I find as an educator, with a PHD and over 20 years of experience as a teacher, principal, and adjunct professor, this method enhances your learning experience. It is one thing to tell someone something and another to demonstrate the skill. Using *The Keystroke Killer* screenplay allows for effective demonstration and transference of knowledge.

Moreover, by purchasing all guidebooks, you save valuable time by not having to read and become familiar with three different screenplays. *The Keystroke Killer* is in all guidebooks. Once you read *The Keystroke Killer,* you won't have to reread it for the next books in the series because you are already familiar with the screenplay. I reference scenes from this screenplay throughout my discussions in the books, to highlight a specific topic. By the time you are finished with all guidebooks, you will be very familiar with *The Keystroke Killer* as well as gain the knowledge presented in each of the guidebooks.

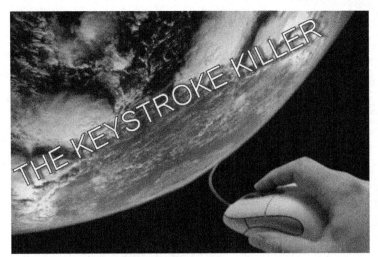

ABOUT THIS BOOK

I'm not going to teach you how to write a screenplay in any of the guidebooks, nor in the comprehensive book. There is a plethora of screenwriting books already on the market. There is no need for me to reinvent the wheel. However, I will take you through the process of developing the topics discussed. After you finish reading *How to Write a Synopsis: Quick Guidebook for Screenwriters*, you will be able to write a well-written synopsis with significance to your screenplay. In fact, you will be able to construct one for your screenplay for numerous purposes, e.g., a business plan, a one pager, a cover, a DVD jacket, and your screenplay or film's website.

After several focus groups, in New Orleans and Los Angeles, the feedback I received was some screenwriters and reality show creators didn't need to learn all three topics discussed in my comprehensive book. They thought it would be fantastic if I gave screenwriters the option of choosing the topic they needed to learn in a condensed format for ready access. In essence, they wanted a *Cliff Note* version on each of the three topics and have the option to purchase only that topic wanted.

They also loved the fact that the comprehensive book covered both screenwriting and reality show design, but felt that as screenwriters, they wanted something that was screenwriting specific without the reality show examples. I listened; and provide them the option with the three guidebooks for screenwriters. Eventually, I'll do the same format just for reality show producers and creators as per their request. So be warned, that is in the pipeline.

Do You Need to Buy Both the Book Series and the Comprehensive Book?

Do screenwriters or reality show creators need to buy all three quick guidebooks in the series and the comprehensive book? The answer is as tall as it is long. There is a Native American saying,

> *"Tell me and I'll forget. Show me, and I may not remember. Involve me, and I'll understand.*

I feel confident that the three quick guidebooks for screenwriters are valuable and provide solid information for the specific topic they desire. They are more of a show and tell in that you read about the subject matter and I tell you what they are and how to achieve the finished product you desire. You gain a solid foundation on each subject matter. The comprehensive book, *How to Write a Logline, Synopsis, and One Pager for Film and Reality TV,* I consider the "involve me" book. This book contains a plethora of hands-on activities to apply the subject matter. This method allows for a true understanding for screenwriters and reality show producers and creators.

Therefore, I'd say it is going to be an individual choice, dependent on how much information you need, as to whether you want to buy all three of *Quick Guidebooks for Screenwriters* and *How to Write a Logline, Synopsis, and One Pager for Film and Reality TV*. You may opt for a combination of your choice according to your specific need.

The Quick Guidebook Series is exactly as the name implies. Each book is a quick reference tool and applies more to screenwriters, as I do not include any samples for reality show creators. Use them in combination or as a "stand-alone" book. Whereas, the comprehensive book not only goes into detail for screenwriters, but also covers how to develop loglines, synopsis and a one pager for reality TV shows. This book contains examples for several screenplays and reality show projects unlike the quick reference guides.

Please keep in mind that I do not repeat any examples from the screenplay *The Keystroke Killer* in the comprehensive book. Instead, I use several references to current films, reality shows, and those I wrote for my examples. This doesn't mean that a reality show creator shouldn't purchase any of the three guidebooks. In fact, I strongly recommend you do so. The information you learn certainly transfers to reality TV shows and the loglines, synopsis, and one pager you will need to create for your project.

I feel using all of my books, is similar to getting a degree – first you attend undergraduate school, then to become more of an expert in your field, and then you attend graduate school to master your subject matter. Consider the first three guidebooks your undergraduate training level course work and the comprehensive book as your graduate level and advanced information for true comprehension and application of learning.

It is my belief as a former educator; the more experience and knowledge you obtain about each subject matter will only benefit you. Knowledge is knowledge no matter how you obtain it.

I feel it is important that I address how I approach the quick guidebooks and the comprehensive book so that you can make more of an educated decision on which books to buy. Being able to differentiate between all of them may be the source of the answer in which books to purchase.

THE MARKETER IN ME

The marketing side of me says for you to purchase all four books; e.g., the three guidebooks and the comprehensive book as well as any other of my books on production and creating reality shows. I have all of them listed in the Appendix. Each book is available at Amazon.com, Barnes & Noble, and other online retailers including my websites. The more knowledge you obtain the more proficient you become. Remember, knowledge doesn't occur through happenstance.

THE PRODUCER IN ME

The producer in me says purchase the individual guidebook book you need to accomplish the task-at-hand. For example, if you already have a synopsis and a logline, and you only need a one pager, then, by all means, you would only need to purchase the quick guidebook on creating a one pager. If you choose to purchase the comprehensive book, you still would benefit. You will be able to hone your logline and synopsis as well as obtain information that you don't get from the quick reference guide on creating a one pager.

THE EDUCATOR IN ME

The educators in me says start at the beginning with the guidebooks, and then purchase the comprehensive book so you get additional practical knowledge on all subjects. That way you work through your undergraduate coursework to the graduate level.

THE FINANCIAL PLANNER IN ME

The financial planner in me says if you can only afford to purchase one book, then purchase the comprehensive book *How to Write a Logline, Synopsis, and One Page for Film and Reality TV*. That way you have access to all of the subject matter. The only thing missing is you won't gain experience from learning by application after reading *The Keystroke Killer* short film. I do find that learning by applying is beneficial. You may want to keep this in mind when making your decision.

WHAT ORDER TO PURCHASE THE FOUR BOOKS

No one can tell you that, not even me. You will have to make that decision based on your current need. I have also written an additional book for screenwriters that assist in the development of a script using your experiences. This book, *Inside the Writer's Mind: Developing a Script Using Your Past Experiences,* is probably the most unusual books I have written because I use many examples from my life on how I created *The Keystroke Killer*. My life experiences include a major illness, a stalker, and going all over the world on a lecture circuit. If you need help in developing your screenplay, you don't want to miss adding this book to your screenwriter's resource library. Available from Amazon.com or my website.

HOW TO USE THIS BOOK

To get the most out of this book please read the short screenplay *The Keystroke Killer* in chapter two. Do not skip over reading it. It is essential that you read *The Keystroke Killer* in order to get the most from the discussions that follow.

For those who prefer reading screenplays online or wish to download *The Keystroke Killer* on their computers or IPAD etc., you may purchase the screenplay by visiting any one of the following websites. Just look for the screenplay icon and click on it.

- www.onthelotproduction.com
- www.drmelcaudle.com
- www.therealityofrealitytv.com

For just $1.50, you can purchase *The Keystroke Killer* screenplay through your secure Pay Pal account. If you choose this method instead of reading it in Chapter 2, you will only need to download it once for all three of the guidebooks; which equals fifty cents (.35) per book. While you are on my website, I have a free newsletter you can subscribe to if you choose.

You may also purchase a bound copy of the short film script, *The Keystroke Killer: The Collector's Edition,* which includes never before seen pictures, graphics, and many more surprises from the short film. This book is available from Amazon.com, Barnes & Noble, Books a Million, and my websites. Also available is the pilot episode script, *Transcendence,* which is more than 60 pages and includes a commentary by me, the beat sheet, synopsis, more characters, and treatment for the pilot episode.

CHAPTER 1

THE POWER OF A SYNOPSIS

"We all now tell stories by cutting from one dramatic scene to the next, whereas Victorian novelists felt free to write long passages of undramatic summary."
Ken Follett – Welsh Author of thrillers and historical novels

WHAT IS A SYNOPSIS?

Your screenplay is finished. Congratulations! Writing a screenplay takes dedication and creativity. Not everyone can accomplish that task. You have come to live and breathe your characters. Every twist and turn carefully calculated. Your spouse and family are relieved because you can now spend time with them instead of the long hours sitting and writing your screenplay until the wee hours of the morning. The drama is finally ready to bring to life and captured on film. Now what?

At this point, some screenwriters feel lost a well as a sense of loss. Somehow, they begin grieving for the special moments they felt when creating their story and giving birth to new characters. They sit back and wonder what they are going to do with all of their free time now their screenplay is complete.

Don't worry if you feel this way too. You'll be busier than ever getting your screenplay into the hands of a manager, agent, or producer. That's the only way it's going to make it to the television screen or movie theater. That is, unless you have the money and means to produce it yourself. If not, you have to get it into the hands of someone or team that can. This requires you to up your game. Just when you think you have free time. Bam! You're not done. In fact, you have lots more to write. I suggest you give your spouse and family a huge hug, a kiss, and a special night out on the town before you jump into the next phase – marketing your screenplay. Time is money.

There is more to write to get your screenplay market ready to pitch. You have to have ready several marketing tools that include:

- A beat sheet (used for development/may be requested)
- A logline
- A screenplay
- A synopsis
- A treatment
- An one pager
- An EPK package
- A business plan (optional)

When you pitch your screenplay, you must be able to hook your audience. Long before a manager, agent, or producer reads your screenplay, chances are they request the marketing tools for your screenplay. The key to selling or optioning your screenplay rests in the power of seven marketing tools: beat sheet, logline, synopsis, treatment, one pager, EPK package, and a business plan.

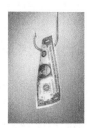

Is one more important that the other? I don't think so. Each, I believe, are equally important. Therefore, you must create each for the most influential impact. That is why it is important for you to obtain this information in this book as well as my others that you can find on my website or on Amazon.com.

For the purposes of this book, it is important that everyone start on the same page in reference to terminology and meaning of a beat sheet, logline, synopsis, treatment, and one pager. Review the following definitions:

- **Beat Sheet** – a multi-page document that outlines your screenplay from the beginning, middle, and end. There are three formats depending on the usage. Mostly used by screenwriters to develop the story and plot of their screenplay. (Topic in my book *Just Beat it! Quick Guidebook for Screenwriters*).

- **Logline** – one-sentence used to capture the essence of your screenplay in tone, theme, and plot. (Topic in my book, *How to Write a Logline: Quick Guidebook for Screenwriters*).

- **One Pager** – a single sheet of paper with graphics used as a marketing tool for your screenplay that contains your genre, logline, target audience, and synopsis. (Topic in my book, *How to Create a One Pager: Quick Guidebook for Screenwriters*).

- **Synopsis** – a one-page narrative condensation and outline of your screenplay presenting your main characters and plot written in present tense. (Topic in my book, *How to Write a Synopsis: Quick Guidebook for Screenwriters*).

- **Treatment** – a multi-page narrative of the plot of the screenplay; which includes the twist and turns, characters and their relationships, as well as presenting the overall tone of the screenplay. The treatment is in present tense. Screenwriters use a treatment to flesh out their story prior to writing a screenplay. (Topic in my book, *How to Write a Treatment: Quick Guidebook for Screenwriters*).

Here are a couple of other important terms in regard to marketing packages for your screenplay or film.

- **EPK Package** – An Electronic Press Kit (EPK) that provides the information on your screenplay in a file that can be transmitted via E-mail. Sometimes, a screenwriter will also provide a hard copy of the EPK for agents, managers, and producers. A budget and financial plan are not included in this package. (Sorry, no book yet! Maybe? Let me know if there is an interest.)

- **Business Plan** – a complex document created to target investors to produce a screenplay into a film. The document is structured and complex. (Available only for reality shows in my book *The Reality of Reality TV: Reality Show Business Plans*).

USING A BEAT SHEET

One of the first things that screenwriters do when sitting down to write a screenplay is to develop a beat sheet. If you don't know what one is or you don't know how to develop one, please refer to my newest book *Just Beat It: How to Develop and Create*  *a Beat Sheet Quick Guidebook for Screenwriters* available on Amazon.com and my websites. Using a completed beat sheet is critical in developing your screenplay and your synopsis. I always use the beat sheet as a guideline when writing my screenplay, the synopsis, and the treatment. It reduces stress because it provides me with an outline. That way I make certain that all elements are included in my synopsis for the screenplay. It really does make writing easier.

If you didn't write your screenplay using a beat sheet, you may want to go back and review your screenplay using my *Beat Sheet Evaluation Form* in my book *Just Beat It*! By transferring your key plot points into the *Beat Sheet Evaluation Form,* you accomplish two things:

1. You make your life less complicated in getting ready to write your synopsis for your screenplay.

2. It is a sure fire method to make sure that the screenplay you wrote is strong and includes key developmental plots included in Academy Award Winning Films.

I was more than green when I first started writing screenplays...I was a high school principal. I didn't know the first thing about screenplays. That was is in 2000. Having earned a PhD in statistical research I set out on my discovery journey to isolate key development points in Academy Award screenplays. BINGO! It was clear to me. My writing partner, at the time, couldn't believe I approached it this way. The only thing certain to me is the method I used to identify the beats. Indentifying beats in a screenplay is that important. Use beats like your life depended on them.

WHAT A SYNOPSIS IS NOT

A synopsis is not the same as obtaining coverage review, nor is it an opinion on the good qualities of your screenplay. Usually, a professional script reviewer will write coverage as part of a company's evaluation process. The resulting coverage document outlines the strengths and weaknesses of a script. You never present your likes and dislikes or the strengths and weakness of your screenplay in a synopsis. You also never include back-story. There are other avenues for this type of presentation and usually is added to a character description in another associating document.

Additionally, your synopsis is not a treatment. They are often confused and used interchangeably. There are two types of treatments:

- Outline treatment
- Presentation treatment

The outline treatment assists a screenwriter to map out the major scenes in a screenplay long before they begin writing the screenplay. It also serves as a way to identify the needed characters prior to writing a screenplay and used during the developmental process.

A presentation treatment is more refined. When the screenplay is complete, the screenwriter or development team modifies the treatment. They match the plot; include the master scene concepts and characters. Then, add it to a section in the business plan or EPK package for use during a sales pitch.

The main difference between a synopsis and a treatment is the length of the document and the usage. Whereas, a synopsis is never more than one page, a treatment is usually longer with more detail ranging from 3-27 pages and written in prose in a story format. On average, a treatment will be between 7-12 pages. It is more like reading a short story rather than a condensed summary that a synopsis provides. Your awareness of this attribute is key to understanding the elements of a well-constructed synopsis.

Most screenwriters make two major mistakes when they write a synopsis. First, they try to include all of the secondary characters. They aren't important to include in a synopsis and the space allotted to one page serves you better by using a succinct narrative of the major plot lines and major characters.

Secondly, screenwriters think they have to include every plot twist and secondary plots in a synopsis. This isn't the case. In fact, if you do, it will not only compound the continuity and flow of the synopsis but will also confuse the reader with what is important. Agents, managers, and producers are used to reading synopses and know that if characters or plot twists are included in the synopsis by a screenwriter, they must have value to the plot. When they discover that you supplied extraneous information, they often turn down your project because it makes them wonder if you know what you are doing. It is best to keep your synopsis to the least number of characters possible. Usually, the protagonist and the antagonist is enough. When an additional supporting character is essential to the plot, by all means, include him or her in the synopsis.

Instead of hitting the head of a nail and driving it straight through, the nail bends and twists and it is difficult to determine the outcome if you include too many characters and subplot developments in your synopsis. In this case, less is more, and more is less.

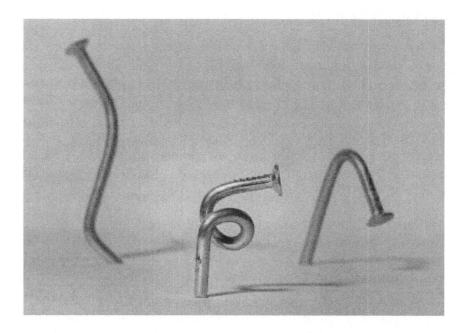

K.I.S.S.

How many times have you heard, "Keep it simple silly." The principle behind the acronym applies in writing a synopsis – keep it simple. You still will have to be creative when writing your synopsis and tell a story - a simple story that flows. To help you get into the mindset or writing a synopsis, I offer you some brief advice. By the end of the book, this advice will make sense. For now, I am setting the stage with anticipation.

A synopsis isn't easy to write. You have to be precise and "short winded." Every word must count. There is no room for extraneous details. Although you will be tempted to fill your synopsis with "fluff," resist the temptation. To counter the Borg Queen, "Resistance is not futile." Your goal isn't to itemize your plot points but to emphasize them by coupling them to your opening hook. You are to write what your story is about and leave out the words that sound like you are reading a novel or short story. Look at the following two examples.

Example 1 – Narrative from *The Keystroke Killer*

> MATTHEW, a New York detective starts the day in despair. There is something heavy on his mind. The morning traffic of the city reverberates through his head as he drives to a park outside the city.
>
> The cool breeze rustles leaves along the running path. Matthew's car pulls into the park. He grabs a pink garden-variety rose from the back seat and walks steadfast to the edge of the pond. Ducks in the pond anticipate their morning meal as the sun melts away the morning dew. Several young mothers watch their children sing, laugh, and play. Laughter echoes through the morning air while BLAZE, a young college student, takes from her brown paper bag a loaf of bread. She begins to feed the ducks as JUDAS, a shadowy figure, stands in a distance captivated by the gaiety of the morning. Smoke from his cigarette filters toward the sky. Blaze's golden brown hair blows from the crisp breeze.
>
> A wailing and ear-shattering scream interrupts the picture perfect moment. TRACY, a small child is missing. Her mother frantically yells, "Tracy! Where are you?" Everyone in the park is on alert. A sigh of relief soon replaces the anxiety in the crowd that gathers around the mother; as Tracy, a beautiful blond girl, age four, emerges from the bathroom. In her right-hand a small container of soap bubbles and in the other a purple majestic wand with silver streamers. Using her "magic" bubble wand, she blows bubbles that float high up into the air. The sight delights the small child. Just before the bubbles burst, Tracy's mother wipes her own tears from her reddened cheeks.
>
> Uneasiness overtakes Blaze. She looks over her shoulder where Judas once stood. Only his smoking cigarette remains.

Example 2 – Narrative from *The Keystroke Killer*

> In the neighborhood park, Blaze, a young college student, finds peace by feeding ducks and watching young mothers play with their children. MATTHEW, a New York detective, stares at the pond with a pink garden-variety rose in his hand. When a child is missing, the quaintness becomes chaos as fear for her own safety replaces the gaiety. Blaze feels insecure as she discovers Judas, who once watched her, is gone. Only his smoking cigarette remains.

Both of the paragraphs inform the reader the same thing. The first one has 290 words and the second has 75, which is four times less than the words of the first. Notice both narratives "tell" a story. Each relates a picture perfect morning in a park where children play under their mother's careful watch. Moreover, both turn from tranquility to chaos as the child goes missing and resurfaces. Both have audience appeal. Lastly, they end in the identical sentence.

The biggest difference between the two is in the "fluff." The first one is full of adjectives and descriptions, whereas, the second is succinct. That should be your goal when writing a synopsis because you have only a single page to capture your entire story. Effectively describe on one page your first, second, and third acts. You don't have the luxury of writing like a novelist. You must have focus in your writing.

To accomplish this task, I offer the following tips:

- Understand the complexity of your screenplay. What is your story about?
- Take notes as you write your screenplay so you can easily identify the first, second, and third acts.
- Identify your very first and very last action in your screenplay. This will help you to bridge your story together in your synopsis.
- Isolate what is essential to your story.
- Write multiple versions of your synopsis so you can take the best of the best.
- Keep the tone of your synopsis equivalent to the tone of your screenplay. If it is a comedy, make it funny. If it is a drama, be dramatic. If it is a horror screenplay, scare your readers.

BASIC PRINICPLES OF WRITING A SYNOPSIS

Basic principles govern the development of a synopsis for your screenplay. I found that the best way to learn these principles is to involve you in observing how a screenwriter writes a real working synopsis from a real screenplay. It is learning through application. That is why I include the screenplay *The Keystroke Killer* and ask you to read it prior to getting into the nuts and bolts of learning to write a synopsis. After reading this screenplay, I will take you  on the journey of how I wrote the synopsis. You will come on that journey as I dissect the screenplay to extract the information to create the synopsis for it. Once, completed, you will be able to use the same formula to create your synopsis for your screenplay.

If you have already read *The Keystroke Killer* and you can answer the following questions, then by all means, jump to the third chapter. If not, it is important that you read it in order to comprehend the principles presented in the rest of the book.

Please review the following questions, and as you read the screenplay, determine the answers. It will make your journey to learn to write a synopsis a better use of your time.

Questions to Consider When Reading *The Keystroke Killer*

1. Who is the main character?
2. How does the story begin?
3. Who is/are the supporting characters?
4. What drives or motivates the main character?
5. What is the main character trying to accomplish?
6. What is the relationship with the main character and/or supporting character?
7. What obstacles does the main character face?
8. How does the main character overcome them?
9. What is that keeps the main character from achieving what he or she wants?
10. What is the darkest moment for the main character?
11. How does the main character respond to the darkest moment?
12. How does the main character overcome the darkest moment?
13. How does the story end?

The above questions serve only as a guide for your reading to make you aware of significant events and relationships occurring in the screenplay.

Now, go and take a bathroom break, pop some popcorn, and get a beverage of choice. Then come back and read *The Keystroke Killer*. I hope you enjoy it.

CHAPTER 2

THE KEYSTROKE KILLER

"I better make the plot good. I wanted to make it grip people on the first page and have a big turning point in the middle, as there is, and construct the whole thing like a roller coaster ride." Mark Haddon – English novelist and poet

DON'T SKIP READING THIS

It is important that you read this screenplay as the discussions in the rest of this book center on the characters and plot in *The Keystroke Killer*. That way, everyone starts at the same point and learns from the same screenplay.

You'll have to trust me when I say, "There is a method to my madness."

ABOUT THE KEYSTROKE KILLER

Genre: Psychological Thriller/Sci Fi
Pages: 24
Screenwriter: Dr. Melissa Caudle
Cover Model: Jamie Alyson – www.jamiealyson.com
Cover Knife and Blood Graphic: Simon Howden
Screenplay Cover: Open Door Publishing House - www.opendoorpublishinghouse.com
Copyright © 2011 by Dr. Melissa Caudle

The characters created by Dr. Melissa Caudle, in *The Keystroke Killer,* are fictitious and not based on any real people or circumstances. Any similarity to a living or deceased person in behavior, character traits, or name, is coincidental. Likewise, the events in this screenplay never took place. This is a work of fiction. All Rights Reserved. Copyright © 2011 by Dr. Melissa Caudle. WGA Registered.

WARNING RATING ALERT

Please be advised that the screenplay *The Keystroke Killer* contains suggestion of violence and is not for the young-at-heart or for those easily offended by the idea of a serial killer. There are **no** profane words, nor does it include sex or nudity. If I were to rate it, I would have to say that it would come across as a PG-13.

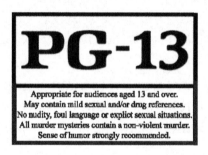

NOT OFFICALLY RATED BY THE MPA

While you are thinking about it, join *The Keystroke Killer* Face Book fan page.

@

THE KEYSTROKE KILLER FAN SITE

The Keystroke Killer
Screenplay by Dr. Melissa Caudle

WGA: 254879456   *THE KEYSTROKE KILLER*   COPYRIGHT © 2011

1.

FADE IN:

1. INT. CAR - MORNING

   Normal road SOUNDS including New York CITY TRAFFIC.

   CLOSE ON A MAN'S EYES IN THE REVIEW MIRROR.

   As the car TRAVELS sunlight begins to spill revealing his face lost in deep thought. This is MATTHEW RAYMOND, 30ish, unshaven, dark circles beneath his eyes and disheveled. Age and stress has not been good to him.

   TRAFFIC SOUNDS soon fade to suburban quiet. The hustle and bustle of the city is gone.

2. EXT. PARK – CONTINIOUS

   Matthew's car comes to a complete stop at a playground filled with FAMILIES and a YOUNG COUPLE in love. It is what you would expect on a Saturday in the park.

   Nobody looks out of place except JUDAS, a transcendence creepy elderly man who stands in the shadows of a tree far from the activity. The forceful sun blocks the details of his face. He lights a cigarette. Smoke filters upwards polluting the sky.

   Matthew exits the car and closes the door. He starts to walk away and then returns to the car.

   He UNLOCKS the car with the remote, opens the back car door and retrieves a freshly cut garden-variety pink rose.

   He takes the rose in his hand, SLAMS the car door shut, and walks toward the pond in the middle of the park.

   Two SMALL CHILDREN lie in the grass and blow bubbles from a magic wand. They watch in amazement as the bubbles ascend high into the air and float away.

2.

Matthew stops at the edge of the pond. He stands and stares as he holds the pink rose in his hand. Caught in the moment of tranquility the morning provides, his reflection ripples in the water as ducks swims past. He bows his head as if to pray. After a few moments, he makes the cross sign across his body ending the moment of prayer. He gently kisses the rose and then tosses into the pond, which adds to the ripples in the water.

He walks away.

BLAZE, early 20s, walks toward the pond with a loaf of bread. They pass each other. Their eyes meet.

A strange look comes across Matthew's face.

Both continue in their previous direction without speaking.

Matthew continues to walk toward a nearby park bench. He takes a seat and watches Blaze from afar. Suddenly, without hesitation, he bolts for his car and leaves.

Blaze is oblivious to Matthew as she focuses on the ducks in the pond.

Blaze opens the loaf of bread; and pinches off several pieces and tosses them in the direction of the ducks. The ducks quickly respond to the morning meal.

Blaze stops and freezes. A worried look controls her face.

A YOUNG MOTHER screams as she frantically begins to look around the playground for her child.

Blaze quickly turns and glances in the direction of Judas.

MOTHER
Tracy, where are you? Tracy!

Blaze turns her attention to the young mother.

Judas extinguishes his cigarette on the ground beneath his left foot. He glares directly at Blaze.

Blaze runs towards the young mother who is now more frantic.

Just as Blaze nears the young mother, TRACY, a small child runs from the bathroom.

The young mother runs toward Tracy, grabs, and shakes her.

> MOTHER
> Don't ever do that again. Something
> bad could have happened.

Blaze stops and quickly glances over her shoulder toward Judas. He's gone.

Only the cigarette remains as small fumes of smoke rise.

3. INT. THE KEYSTROKE KILLER LAIR - DAY

Judas enters the lair and sits with his face to the wall, at his computer desk in the corner of the room. He watches Blaze on the computer monitor as she goes about her daily routines.

INSERT: BLAZE MONTAGE ON COMPUTER SCREEN

Blaze leaves the park. She changes clothes in her car.

CLICK

Blaze drinks a cup of coffee as she works on her computer at a Wi-Fi cafe along with MAG and JENNI.

CLICK

Blaze gets her nails done by a manicurist at a nail salon.

4.

CLICK

Blaze leaves an upscale store.

END BLAZE MONTAGE ON COMPUTER SCREEN

4. INT. BULL PEN – DAY

Matthew sits at his desk searching through files. The sun glimmers through
the blinds. A DETECTIVE approaches and hands him a file. He immediately
starts to flip through it.

BEGIN MATTHEW MONTAGE

Searches his computer.

Eats a sandwich.

Drinks Coffee.

Rubs eyes in exhaustion.

Looks at the portrait of his sister on his desk.

The sun sets through the blinds.

Matthew packs up and leaves.

5. INT. LIVING ROOM - NIGHT

Blaze enters her small apartment. Exhaustion overtakes her body.

She places the mail in her hands on the coffee table.

Her two cats greet her.

She makes her way to the bar, grabs the cat food, and fills the cat's bowl.

                    BLAZE
          You two hungry? I know. I know.
          I've been gone all day and left you
          two to defend for yourselves. Just
          turn me over to the S.P.C.A.

Blaze places the cat bowls on the floor. The cats begin to eat.

Blaze pours herself a glass of red wine and then sits on the couch.

6. INT. THE KEYSTROKE KILLER LAIR - NIGHT

Judas sits at the desk, face in the shadow, as he continues to view the monitor.

INSERT ON COMPUTER MONITOR: Blaze sits on couch as she sips a glass of red wine.

Judas lights his cigarette.

                                        MATCH CUT:

7. INT. LIVING ROOM - NIGHT

Blaze sips her red wine, puts down the glass, then opens and reads her mail.

A NOISE (O.S.) startles Blaze and she looks around. The same worried look as in the park earlier overtakes her face.

                    BLAZE
          Any one out there? Meow Mix ... that
          you? Tiger Lilly?

A KNOCK on the door. Blaze jumps.

Blaze cautiously approaches the door. She stops briefly to retrieve a large bladed knife from a vase that rests by the door.

6.

Another KNOCK.

Blaze jumps again and looks through the peephole. There is no one.

>   BLAZE
> Hello.

There is silence other than Blaze's own heartbeat.

Blaze double checks the dead bolt on the door.

>   BLAZE
> I'm not interested. Go away.

Blaze puts her ear next to the door and listens. FOOTSTEPS.

Her CELL PHONE RINGS. Blaze quickly grabs it from the coffee table. She looks at the caller I.D.

>   BLAZE
> It's you. The weirdest thing just
> happened. (click and static)
> Hello. Can you hear me?

8. INT. THE KEYSTROKE KILLER LAIR - NIGHT

Judas, face to the wall, holds his cell phone. The caller ID matches Blaze's phone. It's Mag.

In the background, the computer monitor shows Blaze as she paces in her living room with a cell phone in her hand.

INSERT ON MONITOR: Blaze puts the long bladed knife gently back in the vase.

CLICK

Matthew leaves the exterior of Blaze's apartment building.

9. EXT. PARK - DAY

Blaze jogs along the path.

Matthew sits on the park bench and watches Blaze approach. He looks like
he has been on drinking binge. His eyes are bloodshot. Yesterday's wrinkled
clothes and a morning shadow beard on his face does not appear to bother
him. The lack of sleep takes its toll on him.

He pulls a picture from his wallet and sadly smiles.

INSERT: Portrait of Matthew's Sister

Blaze jogs near Matthew. He returns the photo to his pocket. As Blaze
approaches, he stands and blocks her path.

> MATTHEW
> It's dangerous to jog alone.

> BLAZE
> Excuse me.

Blaze continues to jog in place.

> MATTHEW
> You're alone . . . a female. Haven't
> you heard? There's someone taking
> young girls from this park.

> BLAZE
> That's an urban legend. I've grown
> up here all my life. Nothing ever happened.

> MATTHEW
> That is until...

8.

                    BLAZE
     Excuse me.

Blaze pushes past Matthew and continues her jog.

                    MATTHEW
     Wait! Hear me out!

                    BLAZE
     Freak.

Blaze looks over her shoulder.

The dark figure of Judas looms through the morning fog.

10. INT. WI-FI CAFE - DAY

Blaze sits at a corner table with MAG, her best friend. Both drink a cup of
coffee and share the same laptop.

JENNI, the third Musketeer of the group of girls, hurries through the front
door and joins them.

                    BLAZE
     About time. We'll never finish
     this project if we are all late.

                    JENNI
     Who said anything about being
     late. I simply forgot.

                    MAG
     How convenient.

11. INT. THE KEYSTROKE KILLER LAIR - DAY

Judas, face to the computer monitor's on the wall, sits and watches several
computer screens at one time.

INSERT COMPUTER MONITOR: Blaze, Jenni, and Mag.

He lights his cigarette that fills the air with smoke.

12. INT. WI-FI CAFE - DAY

A WAITRESS, who carries a fresh pot of coffee, refills the girls coffee mugs as Jenni sets up her laptop computer.

> WAITRESS
> And you? Want some? Of course you
> do.

The waitress pours the coffee and walks away in a huff.

> BLAZE
> What was that about?

Jenni finally has her computer booted.

> MAG
> Not sure, but check this out.

> BLAZE
> What?

> MAG
> Another girl gone missing not too far from
> where you live.

> BLAZE
> Things like that only happen in movies.

> JENNI
> Third girl missing in three months. Same day,
> time, same amo.

10.

                    MAG
I saw it too. The anniversary is tomorrow.
Alerts are everywhere. Check your text alerts.

                    BLAZE
You girls are freakin me out. Just
like a guy this morning.

                    MAG
What guy?

                    JENNI
Yea, what guy?

                    BLAZE
Nothing.

                    MAG
Then just tell us about this nothing of a guy.

                    BLAZE
He was watching me jog and then approached
out of nowhere telling me how dangerous it was to
 jog alone.

                    MAG
Now that's freaky.

                    JENNI
We have to call the police.

                    MAG
The alerts did say to call the police.

                    BLAZE
It was nothing. Really. Now drop it.

Matthew enters the coffee shop.

11.

                    BLAZE
It's him.

                    JENNI
Him? Him who?

                    BLAZE
The guy!

                    MAG
You mean the serial killer!

                    BLAZE
Don't look. He'll know we're looking.

                    JENNI
Because we are.

13. INT. THE KEYSTROKE KILLER LAIR - DAY

Judas, sits in the darkness, at the computer. The blinds shut.

INSERT ON COMPUTER MONITOR: Blaze's empty apartment.

CLICK.

INSERT: A police bullpen with an empty desk.

CLICK.

INSERT: Blaze, Jenni, and Mag at the coffee shop as Matthew takes a seat.

                                        MATCH CUT:

14. INT. WI-FI CAFÉ - DAY

Matthew sits at a table across the café and looks toward Blaze. The girls stare at one another.

12.

                              JENNI
                    He's following you!

                              BLAZE
                    Keep your voice down.

                              MAG
                    Why else would he be here?

                              BLAZE
                    To buy a cup of coffee, like us.

                              MAG
                    We have to call the police!

Mag reaches for her cell phone.

                              BLAZE
                    Let's . . . just get out of here.

                              MAG
                    You don't have to ask me twice.

                              BLAZE
                    The coffee's on me.

Blaze retrieves a couple of dollars from her purse and places them on the
table. The girls grab their things and head out fast. Blaze looks over her
shoulder at Matthew.

15.   INT. THE KEYSTROKE KILLER LAIR - DAY

Judas, in the dark, sits at the computer screen. A black sheet covers the
window.

INSERT COMPUTER MONITOR MONTAGE: Judas CLICKS to different
images.

CLICK: Blaze, Mag, and Jenni rush from the WI-FI cafe.

CLICK: Matthew sits at the table as the waitress approaches.

CLICK: Blaze gets in her car and PEELS out fast. She looks in her review mirror.

CLICK: Matthew leaves in a hurry from the WI-FI café and watches Blaze pull away.

16. INT. LIVING ROOM - NIGHT

Blaze barges through the front door. She looks around and deadbolts the door. She pulls the small table with the vase and knife on it in front of the door. She looks around then goes to the window and double checks the locks on it.

A strange NOISE (O.S.).

> BLAZE
> Meow Mix. Tiger Lilly.

A glass SHATTERS (O.S.). Blaze jumps. She runs and retrieves the knife from the vase. She turns toward the bedroom.

She stealthy approaches the bedroom just as Tiger Lilly and Meow Mix run out of the room in between her legs.

Blaze almost trips, but catches herself as she braces herself on the doorframe. The knife grazes the palm of her hand. It is not bad, but enough to be a nuisance.

A bloody smear remains on the doorframe.

She takes a deep sigh and covers her wound with the other hand as the knife drops to the floor.

She picks up the knife and heads for the bathroom.

14.

17. INT. BATHROOM – CONTINUOUS

Blaze pours hydrogen peroxide on her wound and applies first aid.

18. INT. THE LAIR – NIGHT

Judas sits at the computer screen with his face towards the wall.

19. INT. LIVING ROOM – NIGHT

A bottle of opened red wine sits on the coffee table. Blaze, with an empty wine glass in her hand enters from the kitchen.

Blaze pours a glass of red wine and flops down on the couch. She takes a sip.

She looks at her watch.

INSERT: Watch face set at 12:03.

Blaze stands and heads for the bedroom.

20. INT. BLAZE'S BEDROOM - NIGHT

Blaze throws all of her pillows from the bed. She pulls back the covers.

She walks over to her dresser, removes her pajamas, and then lays them out.

She heads for the bathroom.

21. INT. BATHROOM - NIGHT

Blaze begins the shower as steam begins to fill the room.

22. INT. THE KEYSTROKE KILLER LAIR - NIGHT

Judas sits at the monitor with his face toward the wall.

INSERT COMPUTER SCREEN MONTAGE:

15.

Blaze steps into shower.

CLICK

Matthew lies in his bed as he watches television. He picks up a picture of his sister from the bedside table.

CLICK

Jenni and Mag enter a movie theater.

CLICK

Blaze washes her hair.

CLICK

Fully dressed, Matthew exits quickly from his bedroom.

CUT TO:

23. INT. BLAZE'S BATHROOM - NIGHT

Blaze showers and rinses her hair from the shampoo. She dries herself and wraps the towel around her as water drips down her back from her freshly shampooed hair.

24. INT. BLAZE'S BEDROOM - NIGHT

Blaze puts on her pajamas and climbs into bed. She turns off the lights. She tosses and turns.

25. INT. THE KEYSTROKE KILLER LAIR - NIGHT

Judas, face toward the wall, watches the computer screen as Blaze tosses and turns in her bed.

16.

26. EXT. BLAZE'S APARTMENT – NIGHT

Matthew stands in the shadows across from Blaze's apartment. He looks up at Blaze's window. He pulls out his wallet and looks at a picture of his sister.

27. EXT. PARK – SUNRISE

The sun begins to make peek through the branches of the trees.

Matthew sits alone on the park bench as he reflects on the wallet size picture of his sister.

A garden pink rose, freshly cut, lies across his lap.

28. INT. BEDROOM – MORNING

The sun comes through the beige sheer curtains.

Blaze sleeps soundly undisturbed by the morning traffic and the ambulance SIREN (O.S.) echoes from the street below.

Sunbeams hit blazes face.

Tiger Lilly and Meow Mix sleep curled at the foot of the bed.

Blaze awakes to the ALARM CLOCK. She fumbles to turn it off with her eyes closed.

Tiger Lilly and Meow mix, now awake, demand Blaze's attention as Meow Mix rubs against Blaze's face.

29. INT. THE LAIR – MORNING

Judas, stands by the computer and watches the monitor with his face toward the screen, as Matthew sits on the park bench.

From a distance, Blaze begins her morning jog.

17.

On another monitor, a young woman buys coffee at a coffee stand. He bends and presses the "Delete" key.

MATCH CUT:

30. EXT. PARK - DAY

Blaze jogs along the path.

Matthew sits on a park bench. He picks up the pink rose and smells it.

As Blaze jogs toward Matthew, he stands and hands her the rose.

> MATTHEW
> Please stop. I have something
> important to tell you.

Blaze throws the rose to the ground.

> BLAZE
> What, there is someone trying to
> kill me?

> MATTHEW
> I know someone is watching you. He is called THE
> KEYSTROKE KILLER.

> BLAZE
> I'm leaving.

Matthew picks up the rose.

> MATTHEW
> He killed my sister. She looked like you.

Blaze knocks the rose from Matthew's hand and pushes past him.

Blaze continues her jog.

18.

> BLAZE
> Freak!

> MATTHEW
> Wait! The Keystroke Killer is after both of us. I'll
> show you.

Blaze stops in her tracks.

> BLAZE
> What did you say?

> MATTHEW
> I can show you the Keystroke Killer. He's everywhere.

> BLAZE
> And, I'm going to believe you because... you're a
> freakin weirdo?

> MATTHEW
> No, because it's the truth. You're next.

31. INT. THE KEYSTROKE KILLER LAIR - DAY

Judas sits at the monitor with his face in the shadows.

INSERT: Blaze and Matthew talk at the park.

MATCH CUT:

32. EXT. PARK - DAY

Blaze and Matthew talk.

> BLAZE
> You really believe this?

>   MATTHEW
> He watches everybody, not just you.
> He's watching us now.

33. INT. THE KEYSTROKE KILLER LAIR - NIGHT

Judas sits at the computer, face to the wall, and fixates on the screen's image of Matthew and Blaze.

34. INT. WI-FI COFFEE SHOP – DAY

Jenni reads her book. Mag hands her a couple of dollars. Mag takes the final sip of coffee and walks to the door to leave.

35. INT. THE KEYSTROKE KILLER LAIR - DAY

Judas sits at the monitor with his face to the wall.

INSERT: COMPUTER MONITOR – Mag exits coffee shop alone.

Judas places his finger on the DELETE keyboard button and holds it there.

INSERT COMPUTER SCREEN: Mag dissolves into thin air. No trace of her.

The screen goes black. STATIC NOISE.

Judas gets his coat and leaves.

36. EXT. PARK - DAY

Blaze and Matthew talk.

>   BLAZE
> And next, you're going to tell me
> he is going to kill me.

Blaze's phone RINGS. It's Jen.

20.

> MATTHEW
> None of this is real. You're not
> real, the world isn't real.

Blaze answers the phone.

> BLAZE
> What do you mean Mag vanished?

> MATTHEW
> You're next.

> BLAZE
> You're crazy. Now get out of my way.

Blaze pushes past him and runs away.

> MATTHEW
> (yelling)
> I'm telling you. Unless I can stop him, whoever this is
> or, whatever he is, will kill you next.

Blaze stops momentarily and looks Matthew eye-to-eye. She takes a deep breath; then continues to run.

37. EXT. APARTMENT DOOR - DAY

Blaze runs to her apartment door with her keys in her hand. Her hand trembles as she attempts to put the key into the hole of the deadbolt. After several attempts, the key glides smoothly in.

She UNLOCKS the deadbolt.

38. INT. LIVING ROOM - DAY

Blaze quickly enters the apartment. She looks around as if someone watches her. A worried look overcomes her brow. She locks the door. Double-checks the door's lock, looks into the bedroom and kitchen, and checks the lock on the window. She follows the same routine as the day before.

Blaze paces the floor. She panics. She grabs the knife from the vase. She breathes rapidly in and out and hyperventilates.

She sits on the couch with her head between her legs as she tries to regain control of her emotions to no avail.

Blaze becomes faint.

39. INT. THE KEYSTROKE KILLER LAIR - DAY

Matthew removes his revolver and uses the handle to BREAK through the window.

He climbs through the window.

He scans the room.

Above the desk is a wall with large computer monitors with multiple images of people Judas watches.

He bolts for the desk and searches through the drawers. He looks around the room then sits at the computer.

He moves the mouse and the computer screen on the desk lights up. Most prominent in view is Jen.

The monitor, left of Jen; which has been off, powers on.

INSERT COMPUTER SCREEN:

Blaze lays on her couch eyes wide-open. She is barely alive.

Her white top with blood splatter barely covers her breasts.

22.

Blood oozes from several stab wounds. The long bladed knife with fresh blood lies in her lap.

She tries to focus on the room that is blurry.

>   BLAZE
>   (faint whisper)
>   Please forgive me.

40. INT. COMPUTER ROOM - DAY

Matthew sits with a blank stare as if he sees a ghost.

His left-hand rests on the keyboard and the right-hand controls the mouse.

INSERT: Matthew's right pointer finger as he presses THE DELETE key.

The screen with the image of Blaze goes blank. STATIC NOISE.

Matthew pulls his gun from his holster.

He SHOOTS the computer screen.

Matthew rushes out of the apartment. He is angry beyond belief.

41. INT. LIVING ROOM - DAY

Blaze's apartment is clean and untouched.

No evidence of her, blood, or foul play is in the apartment.

The door opens. Matthew and the LANDLORD enter.

>   MATTHEW
>   How long did you say this apartment was vacant?

>   LANDLORD
>   For a year.

Matthew begins to pick things up from the coffee table and expect them.

He pulls a chair over to a vent. He stands on the chair. He looks into the vent and then gets down. He continues to search the apartment. He searches for something specific to no avail.

He goes from one item to the next throughout the apartment.

He stands in front of the vase. A silver reflection shines inside the vase.

He looks into the vase and retrieves a knife. He pulls the knife quickly from the vase and puts it in his jacket unnoticed by the Landlord.

>   MATTHEW
> What about the girl who lives here? She was just here.
> Her name is Blaze.

>   LANDLORD
> You must be mistaken. The last person to rent this
> apartment was an old widow, Ms. Cavalier I believe. She died
> over a year ago. No one wants to live where a dead body was
> found.

Matthew's cell phone RINGS just as he finds a small hidden camera.

He puts the camera in his jacket pocket.

He answers the phone and continues to search.

>   MATTHEW
> Detective Morrison. (beat). What
> do you mean Blaze Angela doesn't exist? I
> talked to her this morning.

42. INT. THE KEYSTROKE KILLER LAIR – DAY

Judas faces the wall. He sits at his desk as he talks on the phone.

24.

                    JUDAS
        That's right detective. There is no such person.

43. EXT. PARK - SUNSET

Matthew, distraught from the day's events, walks along the jogging path. He
carries a long-stemmed pink rose.

He places it on the park bench where he first sat and waited for Blaze.

The sun sets over the park.

44. EXT. THE KEYSTROKE KILLER LAIR – NIGHT

Matthew walks up to the outside of the Keystroke Killer's lair and stands
guard. If looks could kill, Judas would be dead.

Matthew pulls out his wallet and looks at the picture of his sister as Judas'
shadow passes in front of the window.

                    MATTHEW
        This is far from over.

GUN SHOT.

                                            FADE TO BLACK

CHAPTER 3

THE SYNOPSIS CONVERSATION

"The challenge of "Screenwriting is to say much in little and then take half of that little out and still preserve an effect of leisure and natural environment."
Raymond Chandler – American novelist and screenwriter

SUMMARIZE ME

I hope you enjoyed *The Keystroke Killer* because I had fun writing it for this book series. Now it is time to get down to business – writing the synopsis for the screenplay.

Screenwriters ask me all the time, "How do I really write my synopsis?" Below is a transcript of a Skype consultation I had with a screenwriter who needed help to write a synopsis.

The conversations went like this.

Screenwriter: Where do I begin?

Dr. Mel: That's easy; begin by introducing your screenplay with some type of hook-line. Make it catchy like a tagline. It needs to be a homerun.

Screenwriter: Then where do I go?

Dr. Mel: Start with the beginning plot or the opening situation. Ask, how does your screenplay start?

Screenwriter: You mean the plot?

Dr. Mel: Not really. I mean where you put the opening credits if it were a film.

Screenwriter: Got it. Then what do I write?

Dr. Mel: Describe your main character and what motivates your protagonist. His or her basic conflict.

Screenwriter: That soon?

Dr. Mel: Yes, just like a well-written screenplay that introduces the main character within the first few minutes. A synopsis has to do the same.

Screenwriter: That makes a lot of sense. That's it?

Dr. Mel: No. You have to present your other character or the antagonist and his basic conflict and motivation.

Screenwriter: Now that's it? Right?

Dr. Mel: That's just the beginning. You next have to show the continuing plot and the attraction between the characters.

Screenwriter: How do you do that?

Dr. Mel: By showing the development of the conflict between your characters.

Screenwriter: Then What?

Dr. Mel: Up the stakes for your characters. Relate how your main character gets into deeper trouble and faces obstacles.

Screenwriter: That's easy enough. I wrote that into my screenplay. What's next?

Dr. Mel: Describe how your character reacts and brings resolution?

Screenwriter: Good. I wrote that in too. But, he gets into more trouble.

Dr. Mel: Exactly. He has to fall off the wheel so to speak and really get into trouble. The plot thickens. The basics of 101 screenwriting. So you write that next.

Screenwriter: Then what?

Dr. Mel: Write how things intensified and there seems to be no way out for the main character. A dark black moment for your protagonist.

Screenwriter: I know that too. So, I'm finished?

Dr. Mel: Not yet. Put in some anticipation statement. Make your readers wait for the punch line.

Screenwriter: How do I do that?

Dr. Mel: Return to the initial conflict. Briefly remind your readers what your protagonist faced in the beginning.

Screenwriter: That makes sense. How do I come to the finale in the synopsis?

Dr. Mel: You put the ball back in the court of your protagonist.

Screenwriter: This is overwhelming!

Dr. Mel: You have already done it in the screenplay. The only thing you need to do is identify the moment and narrow it to one sentence for the synopsis.

Screenwriter: Really?

Dr. Mel: Honestly. Then write your resolution and the ending. It could be a cliffhanger, a sad ending, or where your protagonist lives happily ever after. End by going back to the beginning tagline. Make them want to read your screenplay with the power of the words in you synopsis.

Screenwriter: You make it sound easy. It can't be that easy. Is it?

Dr. Mel: In reality, yes. Just follow the formula and you can do it.

The above conversation explains the formula of writing a powerful synopsis.

Within the conversation, the key elements to include in a synopsis are present. To dissect the conversation will provide you with a key resource to write your screenplay's synopsis. Let's look at the conversation with an inquiring mind to identify the formula.

Dr. Mel, during the Skype conference with a screenwriter, taken from her webcam.

THE ELEMENTS OF A POWERFUL SYNOPSIS

As previously stated, a well-constructed synopsis contains basic principles. By closely examining the previous conversation between the screenwriter and I, you can identify the components. The following table exemplifies my point.

CONVERSATION   **SYNOPSIS COMPONENT**

CONVERSATION	SYNOPSIS COMPONENT
Screenwriter: Where do I begin? **Dr. Mel: That's easy; begin by introducing your screenplay with some type of hook-line. Make it catchy like a tagline. It needs to be a homerun.**	Introduce your screenplay with a hook.
Screenwriter: Then where do I go? **Dr. Mel: Start with the beginning plot or opening situation for your screenplay.**	Describe beginning plot or opening situation
Screenwriter: You mean the plot? **Dr. Mel: Not really. I mean how where you put the opening credits if it were a film?** Screenwriter: Got it. Then what do I write? **Dr. Mel: Describe your main character and what motivates your protagonist. His or her basic conflict?** Screenwriter: That soon? Dr. Mel: Yes, just like a well-written screenplay that introduces the main character within the first few minutes. A synopsis has to do the same.	Motivation of protagonist
Screenwriter: That makes a lot of sense. That's it? **Dr. Mel: No. You have to present your other character or the antagonist and his basic conflict and motivation.**	Introduce antagonist and the basic conflict between the main character
Screenwriter: Now that's it? Right? **Dr. Mel: That's just the beginning. You next have to show the continuing plot and the attraction between the characters.**	Attraction between the protagonist and antagonist
Screenwriter: How do you do that? **Dr. Mel: By showing the development of the conflict between your characters.**	Develop the conflict further
Screenwriter: Then What? **Dr. Mel: Up the stakes for your characters. Relate how your main character gets into deeper trouble and faces obstacles.** Screenwriter: That's easy enough. I wrote that into my screenplay. What's next?	Up the stakes. Troubling obstacles presented
Dr. Mel: Describe how your character reacts and brings resolution?	Reaction of main character to the obstacle

Screenwriter: Good. I wrote that in too. But, he gets into more trouble.	
Dr. Mel: Exactly. He has to fall off the wheel so to speak and really get into trouble. The plot thickens. The basics of 101 screenwriting. So you write that next.	Thicken the plot.
Screenwriter: Then what?	
Dr. Mel: Write how things intensified and there seems to be no way out. A dark black moment for your protagonist.	No way out. Dark moment for the protagonist
Screenwriter: I know that too. So, I'm finished?	
Dr. Mel: Not yet. Put in some anticipation statement. Make your readers wait for the punch line.	Anticipation. Make the reader hold their breath.
Screenwriter: How do I do that?	
Dr. Mel: Return to the initial conflict. Briefly remind your readers what your protagonist faced in the beginning.	Return to initial conflict.
Screenwriter: That makes sense. How do I come to the finale in the synopsis?	
Dr. Mel: Put the ball back in the court of your protagonist.	Protagonist gains control back
Screenwriter: This is overwhelming!	
Dr. Mel: You have already done it the screenplay. The only thing you need to do is identify the moment and narrow it to one sentence for the synopsis.	Resolution
Screenwriter: Really?	
Dr. Mel: Honestly. Then write your resolution and the ending. It could be a cliffhanger, a sad ending, or where your protagonist lives happily ever after. End by going back to the beginning tagline. Make them want to read your screenplay with the power of the words in you synopsis.	Ending
Screenwriter: You make it sound easy. It can't be that easy. Is it?	
Dr. Mel: In reality, yes. Just follow the formula and you can do it.	Final Synopsis

This means you can outline your screenplay's synopsis prior to writing one. The key elements presented in the conversation are:

- Introduction of story
- Introduce your main character

- Beginning plot description or opening situation
- Motivation statement for your protagonist
- Introduce supporting character or antagonist
- Motivation statement for your antagonist
- Present continuing plot
- Define what the attraction is between your antagonist and/or protagonist
- Development of plot continues
- Up the stakes for your protagonist
- Reaction of antagonist
- Describe how your protagonist brings resolution
- Thicken the plot by providing a deeper conflict with no way out for your protagonist
- Briefly stall with anticipation and uncertainty
- Protagonist regains control
- Describe final resolution
- Ending

As the screenwriter stated in the conversation, I make it sound easy. With complete explanation of the elements that follow, you too will be able to write your synopsis.

The following chapters discuss each of the above components. By the end of the last chapter, I will have completed the entire synopsis for *The Keystroke Killer* and you will have the knowledge to write one for your screenplay.

CHAPTER 4

THE OPENER

"A story to me means a plot where there is some surprise. Because that is how life is – full of surprises." Isaac Bashevis Singe – Author and winner of the 1978 Nobel Prize in Literature

IN THE BEGINNING

Starting to write a synopsis is overwhelming as eloquently pointed out by the screenwriter's conversation in the last chapter. That is unless you have read this book. So keep reading and gain hope.

To begin your synopsis you will have to introduce your screenplay in terms of style, tone, and theme. This **doesn't** mean you start by writing something like the following:

> *The Keystroke Killer* is a psychological thriller about....

If you resort to an opener like this, you may as well not consider selling your screenplay. It comes across as amateur at best. You will not go anywhere in terms of marketing and selling your screenplay.

What you need to write is something powerful, eye-catching, grabs the reader's interest, and makes them what to read more. After all, isn't that the goal of writing your synopsis in the first place? Why waste your time with a dull and uninviting opener? You must get their attention with the opening sentence.

It helps if you use some sort of hook to introduce your screenplay's story. I find it easier to begin my synopses with a question, so I can circle back to it at the end for my closer. Think in terms of your tagline or a compelling opening statement in a question form. In the beginning, it is much like rolling dice to see what comes up. You keep rolling until you get what you are after. I find it addicting. I keep writing and creating until I end up with the one I think is perfect. That's the power of brainstorming. That's the beginning step.

To accomplish this, think in terms of a powerful conceptual pitch question. Brainstorm as many opening questions as you can for your individual screenplay, then, analyze each one by answering the following three questions.

1. Does it include my main character?

2. Does it reflect the style and tone of the screenplay?

3. Could this be a tagline?

Consider the following examples reflective of *The Keystroke Killer*.

Opening Question 1

> How would you feel if you discovered you lived in a world controlled by one person, who sits behind a computer, with the power to erase you from the face of the earth?

Opening Question 2

> Have you ever wondered what the universe would look like from the point of view of a computer monitor?

Opening Question 3

> What would you do if you discovered the human race wasn't real?

Opening Question 4

> Do you think your world really exists?

Opening Question 5

> What would you do if the one person you loved most were erased from existence?

Do any of these questions sound more powerful? Do you like one better? At this point, it isn't about being right or wrong. It's more likely to be a personal choice. What do you do if you like all of them and can't choose? That's when I go back and ask:

1. Does it include my main character?

2. Does it reflect the style and tone of the screenplay?

3. Could this be used as a tagline?

The first question, "How would you feel if you discovered you lived in a world controlled by one person who sits behind a computer with the power to erase you from the face of the earth?" does in fact reflect the screenplay. It provides the reader with instant knowledge that a person has power over others and can erase you from the face of the earth while sitting behind a computer.

That's strong.   Now I have to evaluate whether the question meets my three question criteria. I have to ask, "Is *The Keystroke Killer* about the power to erase us or is it about Matthew trying to save Blaze from the serial killer?" When I look at question one in terms of my main character, I immediately understand why this opening question won't work. It's not about the power of the killer. It's about Matthew trying to save Blaze. It had the style and tone, but did not relate the plot. Lastly, it is too long to use as a tagline or teaser. Therefore, I would have to reject it as an opening statement.

I feel it important to inform you when designing your opening question identify the protagonist and have an understanding of what motivates his or her actions, thoughts, and relationships.

Do you remember the questions in the first chapter prior to reading *The Keystroke Killer*? The reason I asked the first question, "Who is the main character?" was to assist in developing your opening question. Now that we understand that it is Matthew, we can further analyze the other opening questions.

"Have you ever wondered what the universe would look like from the point of view

of a computer monitor?" is the second opening question presented. I can immediately rule this one out because it focuses on the point of view from the computer monitor. If *The Keystroke Killer* had been about Judas and his world as he watched it from a computer monitor, this question might have served its purpose. This isn't close to the plot. Although it reflected the tone and theme, it was very wordy and wouldn't make a good tagline. Therefore, I have to throw it out too.

Question 3, "What would you do if you discovered the human race wasn't real?" brings us to a different point. It makes the reader look within, rather than toward the screenplay. This isn't necessarily a bad thing because it immediately gets the reader involved. They may even ponder the answer and want to know more. It also brings to the attention that there is a possibility that the world as we know it doesn't exist and someone knows it. In the short film, it isn't clear where Judas is from. We only know he has some sort of power. The power he has or how he receives the power isn't clear until *Transcendence,* the pilot episode, for the television series *The Keystroke Killer.* Matthew has become aware of Judas in the short film. In the pilot episode, we discover that Judas' body was invaded by a fourth dimensional blue energy being that came through an electrical overload when a transformer blew. Matthew doesn't know this; however in the pilot it is shown. Matthew only knows that young women are disappearing like his sister and only he is able to remember anything about them. Therefore, this would meet the main character criteria question.

This question also leads into a Sci-Fi and a possible thriller so it meets the criteria for tone and theme. It also hints at the possibility that the main character discovers that the human race isn't real. When I consider the value this question brings to a tagline, it could work. This question meets the three question criteria and I should consider it as a possible choice opener. Before deciding, I have to investigate the remainder of the opening questions that I brainstormed. So, keep this one in your back pocket, and continue.

"Do you think your world really exists?" as an opening question has a possibility of standing on its own. However, I don't think it pinpoints what I as the screenwriter envision for *The Keystroke Killer* or in the pilot episode *Transcendence.* It raises the question, "Are you living in a fake world?" like the plot of the film *The Truman Show,* or does it reflect the main character living a lie because of others? This question leans toward the tone and theme and it is perfect as a tagline. Okay. It could work, but it doesn't pinpoint the right emotion in my opinion. Somehow, when I read this question, I immediately think in terms of someone marrying into a situation full of lies. For instance, a woman that marries a man and later finds her husband is head of the mob. Therefore, I'd have to pass on this one as my opening question. My motto is, "If I'm not comfortable with it, then how can I expect others to like it."

The final opening question, "What would you do if the one person you loved most is erased from existence?" combines in one sentence some of the good elements found in the others. For instance, it is reflective of *The Keystroke Killer,* both the short film and the pilot episode, in terms of tone and theme. It focuses on our main character by highlighting the possibility that he or she lost a loved one and is introspective which involves the reader to look within their inner self. It can also be a tagline or a form of a logline. This opening is a contender.

Now it is dead even between numbers three and five of the opening questions:

Opening Question 3

What would you do if you discovered the human race wasn't real?

Opening Question 5

What would you do if the one person you loved most were erased from existence?

How do you choose? I look for the question that sounds right. That is catchy. The one question that "hits the homerun" knocking it out of the ballpark. To make that decision, I still have to decide which one introduces my screenplay the best. To aid in my decision, I return to the three question criteria and ask, "Which of the contenders say it best?"

1. Does it include my main character?

2. Does it reflect the style and tone of the screenplay?

3. Could this be a tagline?

That leaves me with my final decision. And ... the winner is ... opening question number five.

Final Opening Question

What would you do if the one person you loved most were erased from existence?

The reason is I felt that it harnessed my main character, the tone, and the theme, while sounding like a tagline. This question effectively introduces the short film *The Keystroke Killer.*

DON'T QUESTION ME

Wait just a second. I'm not finished. What do you do if you don't want to start a synopsis with a question? Then I take the question I like most and brainstorm a statement. I don't have to start over; rather I expand and develop it. Knowing that I prefer opening question five, I start there.

What would you do if the one person you loved most were erased from existence?

I have to think and determine how this question can transform into a statement and maintain the context for *The Keystroke Killer.* I came up with the following statement.

In a world controlled by one person to erase us, Matthew fights to save us.

I liked that for an opening statement for a synopsis and found that it easily converts into a tagline. It is also reflective of both the short film and the pilot episode *Transcendence* for *The Keystroke Killer.*

BRIDGING THE GAP

Now that I have a solid hook opening, I have to think in terms of tying this statement into the remainder of the synopsis while capturing the essence of the screenplay. To accomplish this task, I use a "tie in" sentence or a "connector" sentence. I have to bridge the gap between the opening hook and the rest of the synopsis. It has to flow and above all else make sense. It can't be random.

The easiest way is to answer the hook question is by introducing your main character – in this case, Matthew. Therefore, the answer to my hook question, "What would you do if the one person you loved most is erased from existence?" makes reference to Matthew. I begin by brainstorming ideas. Let creativity flow. They don't need be good while brainstorming. You modify and enhance these later when you write your final synopsis. Right now, your goal should be to get your rough draft for your synopsis. Look at the following connector sentences as they relate to answering my opening hook question for *The Keystroke Killer*.

Hook Question

"What would you do if the one person you loved most is erased from existence?"

Answer 1

Matthew, a New York Detective, tormented by grief, finds out.

Answer 2

That is exactly what Matthew, a grieving detective, discovers.

Answer 3

After his sister's death, Matthew, a grieving New York detective, discovers the truth behind her killer.

Answer 4

Matthew lives this nightmare as he races to save BLAZE, the next victim, from *The Keystroke Killer.*

Answer 5

Lost in shock and grief, Matthew, a New York detective, races to save Blaze, the next victim.

Answer 6

When Matthew reveals the truth behind the Keystroke Killer, he races to save Blaze, his next victim.

To determine which of the six examples best fit the need of my connector sentence, I reread them and reflect on each one. I keep in mind the tone and theme of the screenplay as well as the direction I want the synopsis to take. In a way, I evaluate their strengths and weaknesses.

Examples 1 and 2, don't really work. They leave me cold; and they leave me not really wanting to know more about the story.

Example 3 doesn't answer the question although it effectively introduces Matthew as the main character.

Example 4 does both.

The last two sound like loglines rather than connector sentences. That leaves example 4 as the obvious choice. However, it still isn't quite right. There is something missing. I think it is because I don't know anything about Matthew other than he is a New York detective. I feel it is important to describe him.

When I reread each example, I notice a common theme in more than half of the examples – four of the six mention Matthew's emotional state – grief. Look at examples one, two, three, and five. I must have felt that describing Matthew as grieving was important or I wouldn't have included it so many times during the brainstorming phase. Example 4 draws me in. By adding the grieving description to it, I come up with a fantastic connector sentence.

Connector Sentence

> Matthew, a grief stricken New York detective, lives this nightmare as he races to save BLAZE, the next victim, from the *Keystroke Killer*.

Matthew, a grief stricken New York detective, from *The Keystroke Killer*.

If after you reach this stage in the development of your synopsis and you're not happy with either the hook sentence or the connector, it is time to revisit both until you are. Neither has to be perfect, but you at least have to be comfortable enough to continue writing the synopsis. From this point forward, at the end of each chapter, I include the working synopsis as it develops. The part in bold print, font size 12, will be the new part added reflective of that chapter's topic. The print included in font size 10 is what I developed in previous chapters. That way you can read the synopsis as it develops.

Working Synopsis with Hook and Connector

> **What would you do if the one person you loved most were erased from existence? Matthew, a grief stricken New York detective, lives this nightmare as he races to save BLAZE, the next victim, from the *Keystroke Killer*.**

CHAPTER 5

THE SET UP

"Did you ever see Cheech and Chong's Up in Smoke? That's what happens if you really smoke weed and make a movie. You get two guys and no plot and it's basically like, "Yeah! Let's drive a van made of weed! And that's pretty much the movie." James Franco – American Actor, Screenwriter, Producer, and Author

EXTRACT THE NEEDLES IN THE HAYSTACK

Now that we have our opening question and connector sentence, we begin the next step in our journey – we write the opening situation and begin to build the plot to set up the remainder of the screenplay. Remember that a synopsis is a written narrative. It should read like a short story - a very short. You don't want it to turn into a treatment by writing more than one page. Your goal is to limit your synopsis to one page with three to four paragraphs. Therefore, each sentence you write must translate with power of the contents of your screenplay.

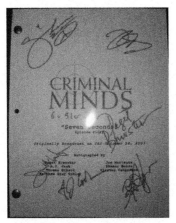

From Dr. Mel's collection of autographed screenplays.

You must be succinct and your synopsis well written. Deciding what to include in your synopsis is much like extracting a needle in a haystack. There is lots of hay straw surround the needle. You must remove the needle and only choose minimum straws. You only can choose a few.

One of my favorite television dramas is *Criminal Minds.* Go figure. I have written a screenplay about a serial killer to use in my book series. Anyway, one of my favorite conversations in this show occurs between Unit Behavior Analyst (UBA) agents Derek Morgan (played by Shemar Moore) and Dr. Spencer Reid (played by Matthew Gray Gubler). It goes like this.

Conversation from *Criminal Minds* (2005)

Derek Morgan: I hate not having a plan. We're looking for a needle in a haystack.

Dr. Spencer Reid: Actually, it's more like we're looking for a needle in a pile of needles.

Derek Morgan: What?

Dr. Spencer Reid: A needle would stand out in a haystack.

The screenwriters for *Criminal Minds*, Jeff Davis, Erica Messer, Ed Bernero, Simon Mirren, Debra Fisher, and Andrew Wilder make a poignant point in this conversation between Agents Morgan and Reid. Writing your sentences after your hook and connector sentence is much like extracting out the needles in the haystack. Why? Consider the construction and purpose of needles. Needles allow for precise regulation and flow of the "material" they guide. There are many uses.

- You can sew with one
- Inject medication or illicit drugs

The information is there. You have to grab it. Be careful. Don't be stuck by it though. Often screenwriters will fall in love with a particular statement or sentence and won't let it go. The sentence is useless if not directed toward the plot or the main character. In the end, the screenwriter is stuck if they decide to use useless words and sentences.

Let the Credits Roll

To narrow your needles in the haystack, begin by reviewing the opening action description of the screenplay in which you need to write the synopsis. Ask, "What is

Jamie Alyson as Blaze.

the opening situation?" and "Where would you place the opening credits if it were a film?"

Michael Hausman, executive producer of *All the Kings Men*, once told me "All films should never have any dialogue in the first scene at least the first three to four minutes of a film." His reasoning, as filmmakers, we need to show the audience action, rather than tell through dialogue. He added, "The less dialogue a screenwriter uses throughout the movie the better screenwriter they are." It is a lesson I have kept close to my heart.

Look at the first two scenes from *The Keystroke Killer* with all dialogue removed. Basically, the only dialogue I initially included in these scenes was the Mother's when she yells at her young child.

Example 1 – Scene 1 and 2 Description from *The Keystroke Killer*

FADE IN:

   1. INT. CAR - MORNING

      Normal road SOUNDS including New York CITY TRAFFIC.

      CLOSE ON A MAN'S EYES IN THE REVIEW MIRROR.

      As the car TRAVELS sunlight begins to spill revealing his face lost in deep thought. This is MATTHEW RAYMOND, 30ish, unshaven, dark circles beneath his eyes and disheveled. Age and stress hasn't been good to him.

      TRAFFIC SOUNDS soon fade to suburban quiet. The hustle and bustle of the city is gone.

   2. EXT. PARK – CONTINIOUS

      Matthew's car comes to a complete stop at a playground filled with FAMILIES and a YOUNG COUPLE in love. It is what you would expect on a Saturday in the park.

      Nobody looks out of place except JUDAS, a creepy elderly man who stands in the shadows of a tree far from the activity. The forceful sun blocks the details of his face. He lights a cigarette. Smoke filters upwards polluting the sky.

Matthew exits the car and closes the door. He starts to walk away and then returns to the car.

He UNLOCKS the car with the remote, opens the back car door and retrieves a freshly cut garden-variety pink rose.

He takes the rose in his hand, SLAMS the car door shut, and walks toward the pond in the middle of the park.

Two SMALL CHILDREN lie in the grass and blow bubbles from a magic wand. They watch in amazement as the bubbles ascend high into the air and float away.

Matthew stops at the edge of the pond. He stands and stares as he holds the pink rose in his hand. Caught in the moment of tranquility the morning provides, his reflection ripples in the water as ducks swims past. He bows his head as if to pray. After a few moments, he makes the cross sign across his body ending the moment of prayer. He gently kisses the rose and then tosses into the pond, which adds to the ripples in the water.

He walks away.

BLAZE, early 20s, walks toward the pond with a loaf of bread. They pass each other. Their eyes meet.

A strange look comes across Matthew's face.

Both continue in their previous direction without speaking.

Matthew continues to walk toward a nearby park bench. He takes a seat and watches Blaze from afar. Suddenly, without hesitation, he bolts for his car and leaves.

Blaze is obviously to Matthew as she focuses on the ducks in the pond.

Blaze opens the loaf of bread; and pinches off several pieces and tosses them in the direction of the ducks. The ducks quickly respond to the morning meal.

Blaze stops and freezes. A worried look controls her face.

A YOUNG MOTHER screams as she frantically begins to look around the playground for her child.

Blaze quickly turns and glances in the direction of Judas.

Blaze turns her attention to the young mother.

Judas extinguishes his cigarette on the ground beneath his left foot. He glares directly at Blaze.

Blaze runs towards the young mother who is now more frantic.

Just as Blaze nears the young mother, TRACY, a small child runs from the bathroom.

The young mother runs toward Tracy, grabs, and shakes her.

Blaze stops and quickly glances over her shoulder toward Judas. He's gone.

Only the cigarette remains as small fumes of smoke rise.

By reviewing the action descriptions in scenes 1 and 2, we can refer back to the initial format for structuring a synopsis isolated in my conversation with a screenwriter. More specifically, "I will have to summarize all of the opening action descriptions into a couple of sentences" and begin to set up the plot.

The first scene begins with Matthew reflecting on his sister's death. He drives through the city into the suburbs. Once there Blaze and Judas, our supporting characters, are introduced in the park surrounded by several mothers who watch their children play.

The visuals presented in scenes 1 and 2 make a perfect place to start rolling the opening credits. The only thing I do is condense these scenes into one or two well-structured sentences for inclusion into the synopsis. At this point, if I hadn't introduced my supporting characters, I would have to do that as well in the beginning section of the synopsis. I not only manage to identify Matthew, but also Blaze and the Keystroke Killer. I'm not always that good or lucky in my screenwriting although I try.

Sample of rolling credits from the short film *The Keystroke Killer*

The Five Ws

To assist in summarizing the action description for *The Keystroke Killer*, I ask, "Who, what, when, where, and why?" in terms of the action description in scenes 1 and 2. Moreover, that is your starting point for any synopsis you write. Look at the five Ws as they apply to our first two opening scenes.

- **Who** - Matthew, Blaze, children and mothers, and Judas
- **What** – Matthew drives to park and prays for his sister, Blaze feeds ducks, children play under watchful eyes of mothers, Judas stands and smokes, Matthew leaves, child vanishes and reappears, Judas is gone.
- **When** – early morning
- **Where** – New York City and in a suburban park
- **Why** – Matthew needs time to reflect on his sister's death, Blaze finds solitude – (surmised from character description), Judas unknown other than he controls the world.

The answers to the five Ws are very revealing. They provide an identifiable guideline, to summarize the action description. It is like having an outline to adhere too. I take what I know by revealing the five Ws and put them together in a paragraph structure. You don't have to write the five Ws in any particular order, just make certain that all are in the summarization. This is the key to writing this section of your synopsis.

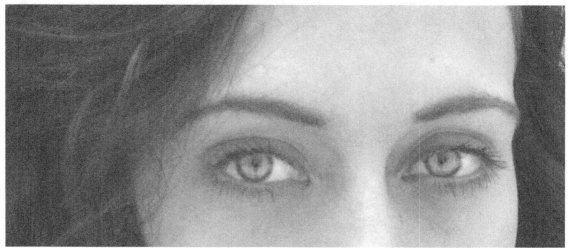

Blaze looks towards Judas - The Keystroke Killer Short Film

Look at the following after I put the five Ws together in conjunction with the hook and connector sentence featured in smaller print.

Example 2 – Working Synopsis to Summarize Opening Situation

What would you do if the one person you loved most were erased from existence? Matthew, a grief stricken New York detective, lives this nightmare as he races to save BLAZE, the next victim, from the *Keystroke Killer*.

Matthew grieves the only way he knows – praying for his dead sister at the park where they spent time growing up as children. It is the same park Blaze, a young college student, finds peace and solitude as she feeds ducks in the pond. As children play under their mother's careful watch, JUDAS, the Keystroke Killer, lurks in the morning mist. It's a beautiful carefree day until TRACY, a small child, vanishes. The mother screams and catches the attention of Blaze. Moments later, the child emerges from the bathroom. Relief overtakes Blaze, which soon turns to concern. She looks towards Judas. Only his smoking cigarette remains as Blaze feels as if someone watches her.

Notice how all five Ws are present in the above summarization. By following my answers to: who, what, when, where, and why; I am able to extract key information to include in the synopsis. I can isolate the needles in the haystack. They are no longer cumbersome and I don't feel overwhelmed. For the first time, I can view them as pinecones amongst a pile of needles instead of a bunch of needles in a haystack. They are manageable.

The next step is to provide more information to the plot by summarizing the events in Act 1. By reviewing the remainder of Act 1, it becomes evident that Judas watches Blaze throughout her daytime activities into the evening. The proof is when the knock on the door and the telephone call scares Blaze as Judas watches from afar. We also get the first glimpse foreshadowing of the prop knife we later discover in Blaze's lap.

Therefore, to add this section to the synopsis I wrote the following plot set up by summarizing the key plot development in the scenes noted.

Example 3 – Working Synopsis to Add Plot Set Up

What would you do if the one person you loved most were erased from existence? Matthew, a grief stricken New York detective, lives this nightmare as he races to save BLAZE, the next victim, from the *Keystroke Killer*.

Matthew grieves the only way he knows – praying for his dead sister at the park where they spent time growing up as children. It is the same park Blaze, a young college student, finds peace and solitude as she feeds ducks in the pond. As children play under their mother's careful watch, JUDAS, the Keystroke Killer, lurks in the morning mist. A small child vanishes. The mother screams and catches the attention of Blaze. Moments later, the child emerges from the bathroom. Relief overtakes Blaze, which soon turns to concern. She looks towards Judas. Only his smoking cigarette remains as Blaze feels as if someone watches her.

Later that day, Judas enters into his dimly lit pristine room. He watches Blaze on his computer monitor as she goes through her day.

That evening, an exhausted Blaze enters her peaceful apartment occupied by her two cats. As she pours a glass of wine, a noise startles her. She double-checks the locks on the door as she grabs a knife from a nearby vase. There is a knock on the door and her cell phone rings. Judas watches from his computer.

Later, if I need to, I can edit or enhance the words. At this point in the development of the synopsis, it is a working copy. Refrain from bogging down with precise words and order. Save this when you get ready to finalize your synopsis. There will always be time. For now, it is important to draft your synopsis one key component at a time.

CHAPTER 6

MOTIVATION STATEMENT

"A champion needs a motivation above and beyond winning." Pat Riley – NBA
Head Coach for the Miami Heat

WHAT IS MOTIVATION?

The reason people behave the way they do is their intrinsic motivation. Some
people are more motivated than others are. In general, it is their innate desire or
willingness to do something. The person propels forward to achieve a goal because
he or she is motive to do so. A man stops and buys roses for a girl he wants to
impress. He is motivated because he wants the girl. Another man stops and
acquires roses for his wife as a way to ask for forgiveness. His motivation is the fact
that his wife is mad. Another man stops and buys roses for his mother. His
motivation stems from the fact he wants to celebrate a special day or simply to

honor is mother. In all three instances there was a man stopping to procure roses. Each had a different; yet, compelling motivation to explain their action.

Motivation, coupled with emotions and driving behaviors such as impulsivity, anger, lust, greed, sadness, etc., is powerful   Everyone responds differently to circumstances they face. It is the "flight vs. fight" mentality. That is why we are all different and unpredictable at best. Our motivation provides reason to act in a certain way.

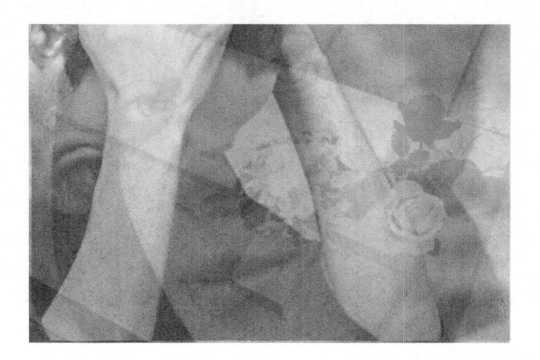

Matthew's motivation is the death of his sister and the desire to save Blaze.

As there are millions of people in our world, there are as many reasons individuals are motivated – lust, greed, envy, love, grief, hate, revenge, jealousy, heartbreak, and more. Something that motivates me won't necessarily motivate you. The love for Antony was Cleopatra's motivation for taking her own life. After her betrayal by her accountant in his reporting of her wealth to Caesar, she was imprisoned. Her longing to be with Antony in the afterlife motivated Cleopatra to poison herself. She became a tragic heroine because of the strong love she had for him. Donald Trump's need for wealth and fame motivates him in his business world. In the television series *Revenge*, the antagonist, Emily Thorne, stops at nothing to destroy others that destroyed her family. Motivated to put food on a table for her four children; a mother is motivated to work three jobs. Indiana Jones is motivated to keep antiquities in museums in *Raiders of the Lost Ark*. Matthew, our New York detective, is motivated to avenge his sister's death.

Unfortunately, most people don't have the self-control to achieve something on their own without motivation pushing them. People ask me all the time, "what motivates you to get up and write every day?" Without motivation, I wouldn't be able to publish seven books last year. Do you know how easy it would be for me not to write at least fifteen pages daily? Some people exercise, I write.

What motivates you to write a screenplay? Is it because you have to have something in writing in your hand? Do you have a vision to receive an Academy Award for *Best Screenwriter*? What drives you to write? Searching within yourself for reasons you do things provide the key to write the next section of the synopsis for *The Keystroke Killer*. This section captures our main character's motivation and internal conflict. Why does Matthew do what he does? Therefore, when writing the next section of the synopsis ask:

- "What is the lead character's motivation behind his or her behavior?"
- "Why does the protagonist do what he or she does?
- "What is motivating to the main character?"
- "What incentive is behind or protagonist?"
- "Is there an emotion that drives your main character?"

All of the above questions ask the same thing only in a different manner. Each one isolates the driving force behind our main character - Matthew. Let's discuss what we know about Matthew. First, we know something is bothering Matthew in the first scene. He drives from the city to a suburban park to pray. In scene 2, He leaves a rose to float in the water. Later, we get a glimpse at Matthew's occupation in scene 4 when he sits at his desk in the bullpen

and works on the files. However, since he is in plain clothes and the office doesn't reveal that it is a police station, his occupation may not be evident at this time. However, in scene 13, when Judas sits at his computer and an insert Matthew's empty desk in a police bullpen on the monitor, his occupation may be more evident as the activity around the desk could reveal police officers.

Example 1 – Foreshadowing of Matthew's Occupation – Scene 13

> 13. INT. THE KEYSTROKE KILLER LAIR - DAY
>
> Judas sits at the computer.
>
> INSERT COMPUTER MONITOR: Blaze's empty apartment. CLICK. Blaze, Jenni, and Mag at the coffee shop as Matthew takes a seat.
>
> CLICK. A police bullpen with an empty desk.

It is foreshadowing. As an audience, we don't know it's Matthew's desk because we have seen him in it. It isn't until the last part of Scene 41 that Matthew's occupation is verbally identified when he answers his phone as "Detective Morrison" and in scene 42 when Judas responds by calling Matthew "Detective."

Take a look at the last part of scene 41 and the scene 42.

Example 2 – Foreshadowing of Matthew's Occupation – Scenes 41 and 42

> 41. INT. THE KEYSTROKE KILLER LAIR - DAY
>
> Matthew's cell phone RINGS. He answers it.
>
> > MATTHEW
> > Detective Morrison. (pause). What do you mean Blaze Angela doesn't exist. I talked to her this morning.
>
> 42. INT. THE KEYSTROKE KILLER LAIR - DAY
>
> Judas sits at his desk talking on the phone.

> JUDAS
> That's right detective. There is no such person.

The aforementioned scenes and dialogue reveal the occupation of Matthew. This by the way I change to a private investigator in the pilot episode *Transcendence*. However, it still doesn't reveal why he is after the Keystroke Killer other than it is his job. If that is the only reason he is after him, then it makes for a dull character and we don't have enough motivation for doing what he does. However, scene 30 provides the audience with Matthew's motive.

Reread the following section from scene 30 looking for Matthew's motive.

Example 3 – Matthew's Motive – The Keystroke Killer – Scene 30

> 30. EXT. PARK - DAY
>
> Blaze jogs along the path.
>
> Matthew sits on a park bench. He picks up the pink rose and smells it.
>
> As Blaze jogs toward Matthew, he stands and hands her the rose.
>
> MATTHEW
> Please stop. I have something important to tell you.

Blaze throws the rose to the ground.

                BLAZE
What, there is someone trying kill me?

             MATTHEW
I know someone is watching you. He is called
THE KEYSTROKE KILLER.

                BLAZE
I'm leaving.

Matthew picks up the rose.

             MATTHEW
He killed my sister. She looked just like you.

Blaze knocks the rose from Matthew's hand and pushes past him.

Blaze continues her jog.

From this section of the screenplay, Matthew's motivation to capture the serial killer, who murdered his sister and to save Blaze is evident. He believes she is the next victim. He is grieving. The motivation of grief is strong for Matthew. Therefore, it is important that we capture this and translate the motivation into the synopsis immediately following the opening question and connector sentence.

To accomplish this task we must state the motivational factor and not allow the audience to guess or leave it for a surprise in the end. Unlike a surprise or twist in the plot that isn't revealed until the perfect moment in the screenplay, you don't want to keep the reader of the synopsis guessing until the end. They need to know this information upfront. With that in mind, we can write this into the working copy of the synopsis. For me, it is easiest to brainstorm the motivation statement prior to adding it into the synopsis.

Motivation Statement 1

A grief stricken detective searches for the killer of his younger sister.

Motivation Statement 2

Matthew, a New York detective, who recently buried his sister killed by the Keystroke Killer, discovers that Blaze is going to be the next victim. His grief won't let this happen again.

Motivation Statement 3

Meanwhile, the killer, known in the bullpen as the Keystroke Killer, has his sights set on Blaze, who has an uncanny resemblance to Matthew's sister. When Matthew makes the connection, he develops a plan to save her.

Motivation Statement 4

Meanwhile, MATTHEW, won't stop until he finds the person who killed his sister. Several young girls have gone missing, from a near-by park so Matthew starts his investigation there. He sees Blaze, who has an uncanny resemblance to his sister. His intuition tells him Blaze is the next target of the Keystroke Killer and he develops a plan to save her.

Motivation Statement 5

The sun rises as Blaze jogs along the park path. Meanwhile, MATTHEW, won't stop until he finds the person who killed his sister. Several young girls have gone missing, from a near-by park so Matthew starts his investigation there. He sees Blaze, who has an uncanny resemblance to his sister. Matthew approaches Blaze. He warns Blaze that there is a serial killer and she shouldn't jog alone. Blaze pushes pass Matthew. Judas looms in the morning fog.

Any of the five statements could work for this section of the synopsis. It will be a matter of choice. When making my decision, I usually choose the statement that best identifies the motive for my protagonist and provides as much information as possible in propelling by story forward. Every sentence you write for your synopsis is directed with that goal in mind.

Statement 1 doesn't tell us anything about Matthew's occupation and sounds more like another logline. Not that having his occupation is important here since it is stated in the opening sentence. The information provided in statement 2 is similar to what has already been said; therefore, there is no need to repeat it. I find statements 3 and 4 provide key information. I also like statements 3 and 4 because of the connecting word "Meanwhile." When writing a synopsis using words to show passage of time help to highlight the story development. Other words to use to develop timeframe in the synopsis include:

- Next
- Then
- In the meantime
- The next day
- The night before
- The following morning
- Later that day
- Later than night
- At sunset
- In the afternoon

Statements referring to timeframe must read as part of a story. It must flow naturally with the storyline. Therefore, I'll choose statement 5 to include in my working synopsis. As the final draft of the synopsis nears, it may come down to editing statement five. It may be too long. I must keep my synopsis to one page.

Example 4 – Working Synopsis to Motivation

What would you do if the one person you loved most were erased from existence? Matthew, a grief stricken New York detective, lives this nightmare as he races to save BLAZE, the next victim, from the *Keystroke Killer.*

Matthew grieves the only way he knows – praying for his dead sister at the park where they spent time growing up as children. It is the same park Blaze, a young college student, finds peace and solitude as she feeds ducks in the pond. As children play under their mother's careful watch, JUDAS, the Keystroke Killer, lurks in the morning mist. It's a beautiful carefree day until TRACY, a small child, vanishes. The mother screams and catches the attention of

Blaze. Moments later, the child emerges from the bathroom. Relief overtakes Blaze, which soon turns to concern. She looks towards Judas. Only his smoking cigarette remains as Blaze feels as if someone watches her.

The sun rises as Blaze jogs along the park path. Meanwhile, MATTHEW, won't stop until he finds the person who killed his sister. Several young girls have gone missing, from a near-by park so Matthew starts his investigation there. He sees Blaze, who has an uncanny resemblance to his sister. Matthew approaches Blaze. He warns her about the serial killer and suggests she shouldn't jog alone. Blaze pushes pass Matthew. Judas looms in the morning fog.

Morning Mist as sun breaks through.

CHAPTER 7

THE ANTAGONIST

"Everybody kind of perceives me as being angry. It's not anger, it's motivation."
Roger Clemens – Major League Baseball Pitcher nicknamed "The Rocket."

THE MEAN GUY

At this point in the development of the synopsis, you have to make certain of two things:

1. The antagonist is clearly identified; and

2. Any supporting characters key to the plot, are introduced.

This doesn't mean that you write something frivolous and say, "And now our supporting characters enter into the picture." Again, this is very amateur. Instead, you make a connection between your antagonist and the story as it develops. To do this you provide conflict through the structure of the plot.

Darth Vader vs. Luke Skywalker

How many times have you read in learning to write a screenplay the importance of conflict between the characters and within each scene? I have been on numerous film sets where the director yells, "Where's the conflict?" and if there isn't any in the scene, he makes the screenwriter add it. That is how important conflict is to include in the synopsis. If it isn't evident, then it's not there.

Most conflict takes place between the protagonist and the antagonist. Seems simple enough doesn't it? Well, not always. Writing conflict into your synopsis isn't easy. It has to be present from the beginning and last up until the final resolution. For the purpose of a synopsis, the best way to make certain that conflict is evident is to state it in the fifth section of the synopsis between your main character and supporting character and characters. Throughout *The Keystroke Killer*, conflict is evident. Let's look at the conflict between the characters.

First, there is the conflict between Matthew and Judas. Judas killed Matthew's sister. That should be enough conflict between our protagonist and antagonist. Nevertheless, the conflict is further developed. When Matthew discovers Blaze is the next target, he doesn't want her to be the next victim. This motivation adds to the conflict between Matthew and Judas.

There is also additional conflict between Matthew and Blaze. She dismisses everything he tells her. The conflict between Blaze and Judas is built-in. The serial killer never directly confronts blaze. In fact, she never meets him and only catches glimpses of him as he lurks about in the shadows at the park. As an audience, we know that he is after her. That is conflict. Lastly, there is conflict within the circle of the three friends; e.g.,
Blaze, Mag, and Jenni. One of the girls is constantly late and they try to provoke

Blaze in the WI-FI café to tell them about Matthew. When Matthew enters the WI-FI café, tension surfaces as the three girls begin to stare at him. The whole time, Judas is watching the interaction.

How do I write all of that into synopsis? I follow the storyline and then summarize it. Reread scenes 10-14 from *The Keystroke Killer*. These scenes present the conflict within the screenplay; and introduce our supporting characters to the audience.

For your convenience, I have isolated the specific areas from scenes 10, 12, and 14 that target the information I need for the synopsis.

Example 1 – Introduction of Supporting Character/Antagonist

10. INT. WI-FI CAFE - DAY

Blaze sits at a corner table with MAG. Both drink a cup of coffee and share the same laptop.

JENNI hurries through the front door and joins them.

12. INT. WI-FI CAFE - DAY

A WAITRESS, who carries a fresh pot of coffee, refills the girls coffee mugs as Jenni sets up her laptop computer.

JENNI
We have to call the police.

MAG
The alerts did say to call the police.

BLAZE
It was nothing.   Really. Now drop it.

Matthew enters the coffee shop.

BLAZE (CON'T)
It's him.

14. INT. WI-FI CAFÉ - DAY

Matthew sits across the cafe. The girls stare at one another.

Blaze
Let's . . . just get out of here.

Now that I have isolated the specific information for the synopsis, I can develop the next section of the synopsis. Like before, I brainstorm several summary statements for this section.

Statement 1 – Introduce Supporting Characters/Antagonist Statement

Two of her closest friends, MAG and JENNI at their favorite study place – The WI-FI Café, join blaze. They talk about the serial killer that stalks girls in the near-by park. Anxiety emerges, when Blaze tells the girls that a strange man in the park approached her. Moments later, Matthew enters. Judas watches the interaction from afar.

Statement 2 – Introduce Supporting Characters/Antagonist Statement

Sitting at the WI-FI Café, Blaze informs her best friends, MAG and JENNI that a stranger approached her in the park. Anxiety builds as the stranger enters. Blaze's anxiety increases and she insists they all leave.

Statement 3 – Introduce Supporting Characters/Antagonist Statement

That afternoon, Blaze meets her friends MAG and JENNI in a WI-FI café to work on a school project. When the subject of the Keystroke Killer emerges, Blaze shares with them her earlier encounter in the park with a stranger. This raises the curiosity between the girls just as Matthew enters. Judas watches the interaction from afar. Blaze is uneasy about Matthew's entrance and leaves.

All three of the above examples effectively summarize the plot points in scenes 10-14 as well as introduces our supporting characters Mag and Jenni. The conflict builds as Matthew enters the WI-FI café in all three examples. In addition, it is not necessary to introduce Judas as the Keystroke Killer since I already have included him in the opening statement.

Does one of the statements outweigh the others? I don't believe so. I think when it boils down to it, the one I choose for the synopsis will flow better with what I have already written. Length will also be a factor. If my synopsis approaches or goes over a full page, I will have to edit and narrow the statement to make certain it fits. For now, I'll choose statement 3 because it provides more information as well as provides a definition of a timeframe by starting with the words, "That afternoon." Let's see what the developing synopsis is now with the aforementioned statement added to it.

Working Synopsis to Add Supporting Characters/Antagonist

What would you do if the one person you loved most were erased from existence? MATTHEW, a grief stricken New York detective, lives this nightmare as he races to save BLAZE, the next victim, from the KEYSTROKE KILLER.

Matthew grieves the only way he knows – praying for his dead sister at the park where they spent time growing up as children. It is the same park Blaze, a young college student, finds peace and solitude as she feeds ducks in the pond. As children play under their mother's careful watch, JUDAS, aka the Keystroke Killer, lurks in the morning mist. It's a beautiful carefree day until TRACY, a small child, vanishes. The MOTHER screams and catches the attention of Blaze. Moments later, the child emerges from the bathroom. Relief overtakes Blaze, which soon turns to concern. She looks towards Judas. Only his smoking cigarette remains as Blaze feels as if someone watches her.

The sun rises as Blaze jogs along the park path. Meanwhile, Matthew, won't stop until he finds the person who killed his sister. Several young girls have gone missing, from a near-by park so Matthew starts his investigation there. He sees Blaze, who has an uncanny resemblance to his deceased sister. Matthew approaches Blaze. He warns her about the serial killer and suggests she shouldn't jog alone. Blaze pushes past Matthew. Judas looms in the morning fog.

That afternoon, Blaze meets her friends MAG and JENNI in a WI-FI café to work on a school project. When the subject of the Keystroke Killer emerges, Blaze shares with them her earlier encounter in the park with a stranger. This raises the curiosity between the girls just as Matthew, enters. Judas watches the interaction from afar. Blaze is uneasy about Matthew's entrance and leaves.

Matthew enters the WI-FI cafe.

CHAPTER 8

CONTINUING PLOT

"There's almost always a point where something happens that triggers the rest of the plot." Jonathan Carroll – American Hyper-Fiction Novelist

THE TRIGGER

So far, in writing the synopsis for *The Keystroke Killer*, we hooked our audience with an opening question, connected it, introduced our main and supporting characters, and started our storyline by introducing the plot. We are heading in the right direction in writing a powerful synopsis. At this stage of the game, it is critical that we develop the plot and provide some catalyst to propel the plot forward. It is easier to say, than to do.

There are two ways to accomplish this task:

1. Describe the catalyst to motivate your protagonist from the point where you left off in your summarization.
2. Add to the storyline a catalyst that complicates "existence" for either the main character and/or the main supporting character.

In *The Keystroke Killer*, the next scene we haven't written about occurs in scenes 16 - 26. Refresh your memory by rereading these scenes in chapter 2. In order to write the next portion of the synopsis, I must capture the essence of these scenes in as few words as possible. Therefore, I ask, "How does the plot develop from here?" I am specifically looking how the storyline develops throughout Act II. After reading scenes 16 - 26, I can provide a concise summary according to the bullet points from the beat sheet I developed earlier. Look at the following examples for this section.

Example 1 – Develop the Plot Statement

Blaze is safe in her apartment after having a difficult day. She stays within her nightly routine by pouring a glass of red wine. Matthew stands below her window staring and waiting to protect her. He pulls a picture from his wallet of his sister. As night turns to morning, Judas watches them both from afar.

Example 2 – Develop the Plot Statement

Later that night, Blaze prepares for bed by sipping a glass of red wine, followed by a nice hot shower to relax her. Matthew's uneasiness causes him to guard Blaze's apartment from the outside. Grief overwhelms him as he looks at a picture of his sister he carries in his wallet. Judas watches them both from afar as the night turns to morning.

Example 3 - Develop the Plot Statement

It's late night and Blaze is safe in her apartment as she drinks a glass of wine. She prepares her bed for the night. Below Blaze's window, Matthew stands guard. His sadness prevails as he looks at a picture of his sister he carries in his wallet. Judas watches them from afar, as the night turns to morning.

The key to choosing which of the three statements to develop the plot rests in the one that captures the essence of the scenes and tone of the screenplay. Please note that I did not include every detail such as Blaze cutting her hand and cleaning the wound in the bathroom. When writing a synopsis it isn't necessary to do so. Keep in mind that less is more.

I like examples 2 and 3. The good news is that I can use either one. One of the reasons I like both of them is because they both show the progression of time. Therefore, I'll choose statement 2 knowing that if it doesn't work out, I can always come back to statement 3 or keep editing until I get exactly what I want in the synopsis. The key is to make certain that I clearly develop the plot without losing the essence of several key scenes. Look at the synopsis with the new development as I develop the plot.

Working Synopsis to Add Plot Development

What would you do if the one person you loved most were erased from existence? MATTHEW, a grief stricken New York detective, lives this nightmare as he races to save BLAZE, the next victim, from the KEYSTROKE KILLER.

Matthew grieves the only way he knows – praying for his dead sister at the park where they spent time growing up as children. It is the same park Blaze, a young college student, finds peace and solitude as she feeds ducks in the pond. As children play under their mother's careful watch, JUDAS, aka the Keystroke Killer, lurks in the morning mist. It's a beautiful carefree day until TRACY, a small child, vanishes. The MOTHER screams and catches the attention of Blaze. Moments later, the child emerges from the bathroom. Relief overtakes Blaze, which soon turns to concern. She looks towards Judas. Only his smoking cigarette remains as Blaze feels as if someone watches her.

The sun rises as Blaze jogs along the park path. Meanwhile, Matthew, won't stop until he finds the person who killed his sister. Several young girls have gone missing, from a near-by park so Matthew starts his investigation there. He sees Blaze, who has an uncanny resemblance to his deceased sister. Matthew approaches Blaze. He warns her about the serial killer and suggests she shouldn't jog alone. Blaze pushes past Matthew. Judas looms in the morning fog.

That afternoon, Blaze meets her friends MAG and JENNI in a WI-FI café to work on a school project. When the subject of the Keystroke Killer emerges, Blaze shares her earlier encounter in the park with a stranger. This raises the curiosity between the girls just as Matthew, enters. Judas watches the interaction from afar. Blaze is uneasy about Matthew's entrance and leaves.

Later that night, Blaze prepares for bed by sipping a glass of red wine, followed by a nice hot shower to relax her. Matthew's uneasy causes him to guard Blaze's apartment from the outside. Grief overwhelms him as he looks at a picture of his sister he carries in his wallet. Judas watches them both from afar as the night turns to morning.

Blaze showers to prepare for bed.

CHAPTER 9

THE GREAT ATTRACTION

"Typically in horror films the character just services the plot, and you really are just going from point A to point B, just so that you can end up at point C. They are just sort of stick characters. That's not interesting to me." Kevin Williamson – American Screenwriter – best known for the horror film *Scream* and *Vampire Diaries*

IT'S MAGNETIC

What happens when you place opposing ends of magnets together? The magnetism causes a force between them that pushes them away from each other. It is the property of the materials, in a magnet, which responds at a subatomic level and creates the magnetic field.

All materials close to a magnet are influenced in one degree or another by the presence of the magnetic field. Some are attracted to it whereas others are repulsed. The relationship is complex much like those between characters in a screenplay. It is the electricity between the protagonist and the antagonist creating an interesting relationship in a

screenplay. How the relationship manifests is key in writing the next section of the synopsis – the attraction section.

As I said, writing the attraction section in a synopsis is much like the theory of magnetism. They are intrinsically related. Thus, if we change the motivation element of the protagonist, the attraction of the antagonist changes as well. We want the protagonist and antagonist to act like magnets in both an electric field and a magnetic one. We want them to be "attracted" to each other. I don't mean in a romantic way, rather, what makes them connect. Identifying the attraction between them is the key to writing this section. The theoretical implications of electromagnetism lead to the development of the synopsis.

During the early 1800s, electricity and magnetism were viewed as two separate forces. However, this view quickly changed in 1873 with the publication of James Clerk Maxwell's *Treatise on Electricity and Magnetism* where he stated that the interactions of positive and negative charges are regulated by one force. What the heck does this have to do with writing the attraction section to the synopsis? Succinctly, Maxwell's theory applies. There is one force, the antagonist, which has both positive and negative influence over our protagonist.

When rereading *The Keystroke Killer*, you discover the magnetic attraction between Matthew, our protagonist, and Judas, our antagonist. Likewise, Blaze also serves as a secondary protagonist magnetic attraction as she is important to the storyline.

We know that Matthew is attracted to Blaze because she reminds him of his younger sister who died at the hands of the Keystroke Killer. However, that doesn't explain Judas', aka the Keystroke Killer, attraction to Blaze. Why her? This question isn't directly answered in the screenplay. It is one of many "topics" my focus group discussed and I predict audiences will discuss and debate.

Judas has developed a pattern as an UNSUB (unidentified subject). *The Keystroke Killer* develops the "magnetic" pattern of attraction for Blaze. However, because this book, as are the others in the series, is based from the short, the attraction pattern isn't as apparent. This does not preclude me from adding this section to the synopsis. I just have to make sure that my attraction statement is clear and to the point. I also look at the beats from the beat sheet. I am well into Act II and moving toward Act III. Therefore, I follow my plot structure and insure I include the attraction between the protagonist and antagonist.

Be reviewing the beat sheet, we know the day has ended and the next plot point begins the following morning during Blaze's morning jog in scene 30 up to the end of scene 33. Matthew, who has vowed to avenge his sister's death is determined to protect Blaze. That's the magnetism between the two. To accomplish his mission, he must alert Blaze so he confronts her in the park. His day begins early in scene 27. He is at the park long before Blaze awakens in scene 28. For a clearer understand, feel free to return to these scenes in chapter 2. Like the other  sections of the developing synopsis, I brainstorm multiple options. So, let's begin.

Example 1 – Attraction Statement for Synopsis

Matthew is determined to save Blaze from the Keystroke Killer. He confronts her the following morning during her jog that she is going to be the next victim. Blaze isn't convinced and discards his warning. The only thing Matthew can think of is to tell Blaze that she looks like his sister who was the last victim of the Keystroke Killer. Blaze runs away from Matthew to the safety of her apartment.

Example 2 – Attraction Statement for Synopsis

The sun rises over the park as Blaze endures her morning jog. Matthew stands nearby and waits for the perfect moment to confront her in regards to the Keystroke Killer. When Matthew approaches, he startles her. He reveals that she is going to be the next victim. She immediately discards Matthew's information. She thinks he is a freak and runs as fast as she can away from him. He yells back to her that she looks just like his dead sister. Judas watches from afar.

Example 3 – Attraction Statement for Synopsis

It's now the morning after a sleepless and tormenting night for both Blaze and Matthew. This doesn't stop Blaze from participating in her normal morning routine jogging in the park. Matthew knows this and confronts Blaze warning her she is the Keystroke Killer's next victim. Discarding the information, Blaze runs away. As a last resort, Matthew yells to Blaze that she looks like his dead sister. Then tension escalates between Blaze and Matthew. Matthew won't stop until he saves Blaze from her fate of death.

Example 4 – Attraction Statement for Synopsis

The next day, during Blaze's morning jog, Matthew confronts her again about the Keystroke Killer. Blaze's frustration grows with Matthew's insistence as she discards his warning. To gain her attention and trust, Matthew tells Blaze his sister was a victim of the Keystroke Killer and she looks just like her escalating the tension between them. Judas watches from afar, as Blaze runs away from Matthew.

Any one of the above attraction statements work for the synopsis. The key to choosing one over the others is whether it reflects the style and tone of the screenplay and captures the essence of scenes 27-33. For now, I'll choose example 4.

Working Synopsis with Attraction Statement Added

What would you do if the one person you loved most were erased from existence? MATTHEW, a grief stricken New York detective, lives this nightmare as he races to save BLAZE, the next victim, from the KEYSTROKE KILLER.

Matthew grieves the only way he knows – praying for his dead sister at the park where they spent time growing up as children. It is the same park Blaze, a young college student, finds peace and solitude as she feeds ducks in the pond. As children play under their mother's careful watch, JUDAS, aka the Keystroke Killer, lurks in the morning mist. It's a beautiful carefree day until TRACY, a small child, vanishes. The MOTHER screams which catches the attention of Blaze. Moments later, the child emerges from the bathroom. Relief overtakes Blaze, which soon turns to concern. She looks towards Judas. Only his smoking cigarette remains as Blaze feels as if someone watches her.

The sun rises as Blaze jogs along the park path. Meanwhile, Matthew, won't stop until he finds the person who killed his sister. Several young girls have gone missing, from a near-by park so Matthew starts his investigation there. He sees Blaze, who has an uncanny resemblance to his deceased sister. Matthew approaches Blaze. He warns her about the serial killer and suggests she shouldn't jog alone. Blaze pushes past Matthew. Judas looms in the morning fog.

That afternoon, Blaze meets her friends MAG and JENNI in a WI-FI café to work on a school project. When the subject of the Keystroke Killer emerges, Blaze shares her earlier encounter in the park with a stranger. This raises the curiosity between the girls just as Matthew, enters. Judas watches the interaction from afar. Blaze is uneasy about Matthew's entrance and leaves.

Later that night, Blaze prepares for bed by sipping a glass of red wine, followed by a nice hot shower to relax her. Matthew's uneasy causes him to guard Blaze's apartment from the outside. Grief overwhelms him as he looks at a picture of his sister he carries in his wallet. Judas watches them both from afar as the night turns to morning.

The next day, during Blaze's morning jog, Matthew confronts her again about the Keystroke Killer. Blaze's frustration grows with Matthew's insistence as she discards his warning. To gain her attention and trust, Matthew tells Blaze his sister was a victim of the Keystroke Killer, murdered by him less than three months ago; and she looks just like her escalating the tension between them. Judas watches from afar, as Blaze runs away from Matthew.

CHAPTER 10

THE PLOT THICKENS

"I began to be impressed by what made a good book – how you needed to have a sensible story, a plot that developed, with a beginning, a middle, and an end that would tie everything together." Dorothy Fields – Film Composer and Broadway Lyricist. Most famous for the soundtrack to *Green Mile*

THE MAGIC BALL

To continue the plot almost requires a magic ball. By this point in the screenplay and the development of the synopsis, the plot is clear. The protagonist and antagonist have formed a relationship. The subplot and supporting characters are involved. Things look good for the screenplay. Not so fast! This is a crucial moment for you as a screenwriter. One wrong turn in the development and it could make the difference to the outcome for all. It is easy to get too comfortable. The biggest mistake I see screenwriters make at this stage is to maintain the way things are developing. They are happy with the progression of the plot, happy with the relationships, and happy things are working out. This feel good moment needs jerking right out from under you to really move things forward in the right direction.

As a screenwriter, you're not happy right now. Remember that! You're really not. You don't want to accept things where they are. You want to throw gasoline on a burning fire not put it out. In fact, you want something worse than what just happened. You must thicken the plot - the most logical course of action. Often, this is a calculated risk the screenwriter provides for the protagonist to tackle and confront. The protagonist must feel doubtful of his course of action, or whether obstacles thrown at him, can be overturned. The same holds true when developing the synopsis at this stage. Like the screenplay, the synopsis must describe the plot thickening.

The Keystroke Killer follows the same pattern; therefore, so should the synopsis. Beginning in scene 31 is the point at which the audience gets a glimpse to how the serial killer murders his victims. Look at the following taken from scenes 31, 33, 34, and 35 to make my point.

Example 1 – Scenes 31, 33, 34, 35 - Inserts from *The Keystroke Killer*

31. INT. THE KEYSTROKE KILLER LAIR - NIGHT

Judas at the computer.

33. INT. THE KEYSTROKE KILLER LAIR – NIGHT

Judas sits at the computer and fixates on the screen's image of Matthew and Blaze.

34. INT. WI-FI COFFEE SHOP – DAY

Jenni reads her book. Mag hands her a couple of dollars for her coffee.

Mag takes the final sip and walks to the door to leave.

35. INT. THE KEYSTROKE KILLER LAIR - DAY

Judas sits at the monitor.

INSERT: COMPUTER MONITOR – Mag exits coffee shop alone.

The plot has now thickened. It brings the question, "Why is Judas watching Mag and Jenni when they aren't with Blaze?" Moreover, a bigger question, why isn't he keeping a closer eye on Blaze and Matthew while they talk at the park? Therefore, we add to our synopsis this turn in events.

Statement 1 -The Plot Thickens

Meanwhile, Mag and Jenni wait for Blaze at the WI-FI café. As Judas watches Mag and Jenni, he keeps a close watch on the conversation between Matthew and Blaze.

Statement 2 – The Plot Thickens

Judas keeps a close watch from afar on the conversation between Matthew and Blaze. Meanwhile, Mag and Jenni wait for Blaze at the WI-FI café.

Statement 3 - The Plot Thickens

Matthew continues to convince Blaze that she is the next victim of the Keystroke Killer while Mag and Jenni wait impatiently at the WI-FI café. Judas keeps all under surveillance.

Each statement works for the synopsis. All capture the tone and essence of the screenplay. Because length of the synopsis is a concern, I'll choose the shortest one – statement 2 and add it to the working synopsis.

Working Synopsis with the Plot Thickens Statement Added

What would you do if the one person you loved most were erased from existence? MATTHEW, a grief stricken New York detective, lives this nightmare as he races to save BLAZE, the next victim, from the KEYSTROKE KILLER.

Matthew grieves the only way he knows – praying for his dead sister at the park where they spent time growing up as children. It is the same park Blaze, a young college student, finds peace and solitude as she feeds ducks in the pond. As children play under their mother's careful watch, JUDAS, aka the Keystroke Killer, lurks in the morning mist. It's a beautiful carefree day until TRACY, a small child, vanishes. The MOTHER screams which catches the attention of Blaze. Moments later, the child emerges from the bathroom. Relief overtakes Blaze, which soon turns to concern. She looks towards Judas. Only his smoking cigarette remains as Blaze feels as if someone watches her.

The sun rises as Blaze jogs along the park path. Meanwhile, Matthew, won't stop until he finds the person who killed his sister. Several young girls have gone missing, from a near-by park so Matthew starts his investigation there. He sees Blaze, who has an uncanny resemblance to his deceased sister. Matthew approaches Blaze. He warns her about the serial killer and suggests she shouldn't jog alone. Blaze pushes past Matthew. Judas looms in the morning fog.

That afternoon, Blaze meets her friends MAG and JENNI in a WI-FI café to work on a school project. When the subject of the Keystroke Killer emerges, Blaze shares her earlier encounter in the park with a stranger. This raises the curiosity between the girls just as Matthew, enters. Judas watches the interaction from afar. Blaze is uneasy about Matthew's entrance and leaves.

Later that night, Blaze prepares for bed by sipping a glass of red wine, followed by a nice hot shower to relax her. Matthew's uneasy causes him to guard Blaze's apartment from the outside. Grief overwhelms him as he looks at a picture of his sister he carries in his wallet. Judas watches them both from afar as the night turns to morning.

The next day, during Blaze's morning jog, Matthew confronts her again about the Keystroke Killer. Blaze's frustration grows with Matthew's insistence as she discards his warning. To gain her attention and trust, Matthew tells Blaze his sister was a victim of the Keystroke Killer, murdered by him less than three months ago; and she looks just like her escalating the tension between them. Judas watches from afar, as Blaze runs away from Matthew.

Judas keeps a close watch from afar on the conversation between Matthew and Blaze. Meanwhile, Mag and Jenni wait for Blaze at the WI-FI café.

CHAPTER 11

UP THE STAKES

THE KEYSTROKE KILLER
"Up the Stakes"

"Those who plot the destruction of others often perish in the attempt." Thomas
Moore – American Writer and Psychotherapist – best known for the book *Care of the Soul*

THE IMPOSSIBLE SITUATION

Just when the protagonist has things under control, the screenwriter throws a
monkey-wrench into the plot. The stakes get higher and more complicated.
Someone will perish. This strategy is one of the basics for all great screenwriting.
The same holds true when writing the synopsis. Therefore, it is necessary to
identify the monkey wrench.

For some screenplays, the monkey wrench is easier to identify. It should be evident
when you review the beat sheet. If this key element is missing in your screenplay, I
strongly suggest that you rewrite it to strengthen your plot.

In *The Keystroke Killer*, I up the stakes in a variety of situations. The first one occurs when Mag gets tired of waiting on Blaze in the WI-FI café and leaves. Judas watches and he presses the "Delete" key on his keyboard. As a result, Mag vanishes. It is a cause and effect situation, which foreshadows how Judas kills his victims. This scene sets up the remainder of the screenplay as tension builds. Look at the scene 35 from where we left off in the last section.

Example from *The Keystroke Killer* – Scene 35

> 35. INT. THE KEYSTROKE KILLER LAIR - DAY
>
> Judas sits at the monitor.
>
> INSERT: COMPUTER MONITOR – Mag exits coffee shop alone.
>
> Judas places his finger on the DELETE button on the keyboard and holds it there.
>
> INSERT COMPUTER SCREEN: Mag dissolves into thin air. No trace of her.
>
> The screen goes black. STATIC NOISE.
>
> Judas gets his coat and leaves.

The plot is now thicker than before. At this point, neither Matthew nor Blaze is aware of Mag's disappearance. As Blaze begins to run from Matthew, she learns of Mag's disappearance when Jenni calls her. We are not sure where Judas is heading when he leaves his lair. He could be on his way to the WI-FI café, to Matthew's work, or to Blaze's apartment. This uncertainty adds to the plot and heightens the tension level the audience feels. As the new development unfolds, add it next to the synopsis. Look at the following statements that describe how the stakes begin to mount for Matthew.

Statement 1 – Up the Stakes

> Mag leaves the WI-FI café out of frustration. She's tired of waiting on Blaze. Under the careful watch of Judas, Blaze and Matthew continue their

conversation.   Judas presses the "Delete" key on the keyboard.   Mag vanishes."

Statement 2 – Up the Stakes

Mag dissolves into thin air as she leaves the WI-FI café. Judas is in control as he maintains is watch on the conversation between Blaze and Matthew. Blaze's phone rings.

Statement 3 – Up the Stakes

Judas presses the "Delete" key on the keyboard as Mag, who leaves the WI-FI café dissolves into thin air. There is no trace of her. Judas leaves to a non-disclosed location. Shortly after, Blaze's cell phone rings.

I think statement 3 works best; therefore, I'll add it to the working synopsis.

Working Synopsis with Up the Stakes Statement Added

What would you do if the one person you loved most were erased from existence? MATTHEW, a grief stricken New York detective, lives this nightmare as he races to save BLAZE, the next victim, from the KEYSTROKE KILLER.

Matthew grieves the only way he knows – praying for his dead sister at the park where they spent time growing up as children. It is the same park Blaze, a young college student, finds peace and solitude as she feeds ducks in the pond. As children play under their mother's careful watch, JUDAS, aka the Keystroke Killer, lurks in the morning mist. It's a beautiful carefree day until TRACY, a small child, vanishes. The MOTHER screams which catches the attention of Blaze. Moments later, the child emerges from the bathroom. Relief overtakes Blaze, which soon turns to concern. She looks towards Judas. Only his smoking cigarette remains as Blaze feels as if someone watches her.

The sun rises as Blaze jogs along the park path. Meanwhile, Matthew, won't stop until he finds the person who killed his sister. Several young girls have gone missing, from a near-by park so Matthew starts his investigation there. He sees Blaze, who has an uncanny resemblance to his deceased sister. Matthew approaches Blaze. He warns her about the serial killer and suggests she shouldn't jog alone. Blaze pushes past Matthew. Judas looms in the morning fog.

That afternoon, Blaze meets her friends MAG and JENNI in a WI-FI café to work on a school project. When the subject of the Keystroke Killer emerges, Blaze shares her earlier encounter in the park with a stranger. This raises the curiosity between the girls just as Matthew, enters. Judas watches the interaction from afar. Blaze is uneasy about Matthew's entrance and leaves.

Later that night, Blaze prepares for bed by sipping a glass of red wine, followed by a nice hot shower to relax her. Matthew's uneasy causes him to guard Blaze's apartment from the outside. Grief overwhelms him as he looks at a picture of his sister he carries in his wallet. Judas watches them both from afar as the night turns to morning.

The next day, during Blaze's morning jog, Matthew confronts her again about the Keystroke Killer. Blaze's frustration grows with Matthew's insistence as she discards his warning. To gain her attention and trust, Matthew tells Blaze his sister was a victim of the Keystroke Killer, murdered by him less than three months ago; and she looks just like her escalating the tension between them. Judas watches from afar, as Blaze runs away from Matthew.

Judas keeps a close watch from afar on the conversation between Matthew and Blaze. Meanwhile, Mag and Jenni wait for Blaze at the WI-FI café.

Judas presses the "Delete" key on the keyboard as Mag, who leaves the WI-FI café, dissolves into thin air. There is no trace of her. Judas leaves to a non-disclosed location. Shortly after, Blaze's cell phone rings.

CHAPTER 12

REACTION

"We began to do little things, have little scenes where we just talked about things that had nothing to do with the plot. In fact, in the beginning, they didn't want us to do that. But as time went on, you see that in so many shows. I think we were the first to do that." Don Knotts – American Actor – best known as Barney Fife on the late 1960s sitcom The Andy Griffith Show

ACTION CAUSES REACTION

With any cause and effect, there is a reaction. Newton's Laws of Motion states, "Every object persists in its state of rest or uniform motion in a straight line unless it is compelled to change that state by forces impressed on it." Newton's law can easily apply to the next section of our synopsis. For example, any time the antagonist throws something at the protagonist, the protagonist reacts. When the protagonist is close to solving the problem, the antagonist reacts again and throws more his way.

The way the protagonist reacts is important in our plot development and in writing a synopsis. In *The Keystroke Killer*, Matthew reacts at every twist and turn Judas throws his way. After Judas kills Matthew's sister, he is hell bent on taking him down. He'll stop at nothing to find Judas and races to save Blaze. Then, when Blaze won't listen to him, he comes at her with more details and facts. Only after Blaze receives Jenni's phone call, does she consider Matthew's point of view. As the screenwriter, I don't confirm or state this point directly in the screenplay. Again, I provide another topic of conversation for the focus group and you. When she stops in her tracks and looks Matthew in his eyes – what was she thinking? She could be thinking that Matthew may be telling the truth.

To include the reaction statement in the synopsis you must pinpoint the exact scene or moment that the protagonist reacts after the stakes are higher. In *The Keystroke Killer*, that moment occurs in scene 36. Look at that moment from the screenplay.

Example – Scene 36 from *The Keystroke Killer*

      36. EXT. PARK - DAY

        Blaze and Matthew talk.

                    BLAZE
          And next, you're going to tell me
          he's going to kill me.

        Blaze's phone RINGS. It's Jen.

                  MATTHEW
          None of this is real. You're not
          real, the world isn't real.

        Blaze answers the phone.

                  BLAZE
        What do you mean Mag vanished?

> MATTHEW
> You're next.

> BLAZE
> You're crazy. Now get out of my way.

Blaze pushes past him and runs away.

> MATTHEW
> (yelling)
> I'm telling you. If I don't find him first, whoever
> this is or whatever he is, he is going to kill you next.

Blaze stops momentarily and looks Matthew eye-to-eye. She takes a deep breath, then continues to run.

Brainstorming a reaction statement is to summarize the moment in the screenplay that it occurs. Look at the following options for the synopsis.

Statement 1 – Reaction Statement

Time is running short to save Blaze from the Keystroke Killer leaving Matthew with no other choice but to reveal the truth that the world as we know it isn't real. Blaze panics when Jenni calls to inform her that Mag has vanished. Matthew confirms his belief by insisting he can show Blaze the truth. Blaze bolts for safety.

Statement 2 – Reaction Statement

Matthew and Blaze continue their conversation. When Matthew tells Blaze the world isn't real, she panics. Determined to save her from the Keystroke Killer, Matthew is more persistent. He tells Blaze he can show her the truth. Blaze runs from him after receiving a phone call from Jenni informing her Mag has vanished.

Statement 3 – Reaction Statement

Moments later, Matthew is more determined to rescue Blaze than before. After Blaze receives a phone call from Jenni telling her Mag has vanished, panic overcomes Blaze leaving Matthew to expose the truth about an unknown reality of the world created by the Keystroke Killer. Nothing will convince Blaze as she pushes past Matthew.

Adding the reaction statement to the synopsis brings clarity to the plot. Look at the working synopsis up to this point in development with reaction statement 3 added.

Working Synopsis with Reaction Statement Added

What would you do if the one person you loved most were erased from existence? MATTHEW, a grief stricken New York detective, lives this nightmare as he races to save BLAZE, the next victim, from the KEYSTROKE KILLER.

Matthew grieves the only way he knows – praying for his dead sister at the park where they spent time growing up as children. It is the same park Blaze, a young college student, finds peace and solitude as she feeds ducks in the pond. As children play under their mother's careful watch, JUDAS, aka the Keystroke Killer, lurks in the morning mist. It's a beautiful carefree day until TRACY, a small child, vanishes. The MOTHER screams which catches the attention of Blaze. Moments later, the child emerges from the bathroom. Relief overtakes Blaze, which soon turns to concern. She looks towards Judas. Only his smoking cigarette remains as Blaze feels as if someone watches her.

The sun rises as Blaze jogs along the park path. Meanwhile, Matthew, won't stop until he finds the person who killed his sister. Several young girls have gone missing, from a near-by park so Matthew starts his investigation there. He sees Blaze, who has an uncanny resemblance to his deceased sister. Matthew approaches Blaze. He warns her about the serial killer and suggests she shouldn't jog alone. Blaze pushes past Matthew. Judas looms in the morning fog.

That afternoon, Blaze meets her friends MAG and JENNI in a WI-FI café to work on a school project. When the subject of the Keystroke Killer emerges, Blaze shares her earlier encounter in the park with a stranger. This raises the curiosity between the girls just as Matthew, enters. Judas watches the interaction from afar. Blaze is uneasy about Matthew's entrance and leaves.

Later that night, Blaze prepares for bed by sipping a glass of red wine, followed by a nice hot shower to relax her. Matthew's uneasy causes him to guard Blaze's apartment from the outside. Grief overwhelms him as he looks at a picture of his sister he carries in his wallet. Judas watches them both from afar as the night turns to morning.

The next day, during Blaze's morning jog, Matthew confronts her again about the Keystroke Killer. Blaze's frustration grows with Matthew's insistence as she discards his warning. To gain her attention and trust, Matthew tells Blaze his sister was a victim of the Keystroke Killer, murdered by him less than three months ago; and she looks just like her escalating the tension between them. Judas watches from afar, as Blaze runs away from Matthew.

Judas keeps a close watch from afar on the conversation between Matthew and Blaze. Meanwhile, Mag and Jenni wait for Blaze at the WI-FI café.

Judas presses the "Delete" key on the keyboard as Mag, who leaves the WI-FI café, dissolves into thin air. There is no trace of her. Judas leaves to a non-disclosed location. Shortly after, Blaze's cell phone rings.

Moments later, Matthew is more determined to rescue Blaze than before. After Blaze receives a phone call from Jenni telling her Mag has vanished, panic overcomes her leaving Matthew to expose the truth about an unknown reality of the world created by the Keystroke Killer. Nothing will convince Blaze as she pushes past Matthew.

Outside of cafe where Mag vanishes.

CHAPTER 13

BRINGING RESOLUTION

"Essentially and most simply put, plot is what the characters do to deal with the situation they are in. It is a logical sequence of events that grow from an initial incident that alters the status quo of the characters." Elizabeth George – American Novelist of psychological suspense genre

ALTERING THE STATUS QUO

Is anybody ever truly happy all the time? I hope not. What a dull world we would live in if that were the case. Likewise, are you happy with the status quo? I know I'm not. At this stage of writing a synopsis, you start considering how you will bring the plot to the end.

You have to know how you will tie up the loose ends. It has to be a graceful denouement after Matthew's attempt to get Blaze on his side fails. Without doubt, Matthew feels grief. That's a given and basic realization for *The Keystroke Killer* screenplay. He races to save Blaze. He knows the world isn't real. Mag has vanished. Matthew has to convince Blaze or she will face the consequences of the Keystroke Killer.

I have to resist the urge for Blaze and Matthew to fall in love. This isn't a love story – it's a psychological sci-fi thriller that requires a complicated plot followed by a complicated resolution. The story is over if Matthew captures the Keystroke Killer or Blaze agrees with him. Where does this leave us in our plot development? As screenwriters, do we alter the status quo by daring to be different? Of course we do.

Finding a resolution doesn't mean it meets expectations of the status quo. In fact, when it shakes things up – the resolution has more impact and meaning. The perfect example is the 2011 film *Young Adult* by Diablo Cody, screenwriter of *Juno*. This film defies the Hollywood traditional expected ending. I like that. In fact, I love it. Therefore, I say go for it in an unusual and unexpected fashion. Get "Jiggy" with it so to speak and shake up the status quo as the screenwriter. You do have that power.

THE MEDIATOR

Mediation between parties in dispute appeared in very ancient times. The practice developed in Ancient Greece found its way into Roman civilization with dictated laws for the population. Early cultures regarded mediators as a sacred figure and each treated with the utmost respect. During the last decade mediation, as used in law, has become a very popular approach to resolve

Parthenon in Athens Greece

conflicts between two or more parties. A mediator, a neutral third party, negotiates between the parties to bring a resolution instead of a court trial. The presence of the mediator is essential in the mediation process and they tap into various techniques to open and improve dialogue between the conflicting parties. The mediator must have the respect of all conflicting parties or it won't work.

When there is a major impact and the storyline requires mediation, the character you bring to the mediation table will be an important decision for you as the screenwriter. You must decide who will have a major impact on whether the mediation succeeds or falters. What does this have to do with *The Keystroke Killer*? That's a fair question.

Who is the mediator in *The Keystroke Killer*? It can't be Matthew. He's our protagonist. It's not Judas because he's the killer. Blaze is out of the question because she is the target. In this situation, the mediator is the audience. We start to fall into alignment with one of these characters. This may or may not seem obvious to you. There are important tactical considerations when choosing.

If you fall in line with Matthew, then it's obvious that you want him to succeed. The resolution for him is to catch the Keystroke Killer before he kills Blaze. Blaze's supporters lean toward wanting Blaze to get as far away as possible from Matthew. She must save herself and Matthew won't have anything to do with whether she lives or dies. In fact, many suspect Matthew as the killer and not Judas. Judas supporters have the strong urge for him to succeed and maintain control over others. He created the world, so he maintains it according to his standard. It is a cat and mouse game where the mice play regardless of the location of the cat in the dog eat dog world Judas orchestrates.

Whomever you choose as the mediator complicates the plot for *The Keystroke Killer.* The only knowledge we have that is certain is we have to bring resolution to the plot and create an ending worthy of the first two acts.

In review, the Hollywood structure of a screenplay is a three-act structure. This format is easy for the audience to understand and to identify the elements of a plot. The first act introduces the characters and sets up the plot. It structures the remainder of the screenplay by making us comfortable with the theme and context. In the second act, our emotions heighten and we are committed to the story. We feel as if we know the protagonist and know what drives the antagonist. We ultimately take sides whether we do so consciously or subconsciously. We make a decision as an audience member – we are the mediator. The third act brings closure and wraps the story. Sometimes, the closure is met with satisfactory ratings, whereas, others leave us with disappointment.

Act I, is about 30 pages, Act II is 60 pages, and Act III is an additional 30 pages for a feature length film. For a short film, Act I is about three pages, Act II is 12 pages, and Act II is the remaining pages. The inciting incident and beginning of the plot occurs in Act I. In Act II, the plot thickens and develops. Then, the climax and final image of the story occurs in Act III.

As a screenwriter, we don't reveal the resolution all at once or we'll disappoint our mediator and lose momentum. Therefore, we must take baby steps and ease into the resolution. Applying this advice to *The Keystroke Killer's* synopsis, I can write a beginning resolution statement to add to the developing synopsis. To isolate the subject matter for the resolution statement, I refer to my beat sheet and the screenplay. The following scene isolates how Matthew, our protagonist, begins to bring resolution to the conflict and provide the audience the influence of a third party mediator.

Look at the beginning of scene 39 from *The Keystroke Killer*. In response to Judas having "Deleted" Mag, Matthew takes action by going to the lair. This portion of scene 39 identifies the resolution from Matthew's point of view.

Example – Scene 39 from *The Keystroke Killer*

> 39. INT. THE KEYSTROKE KILLER LAIR - DAY
>
> Matthew grabs his revolver and uses it to BREAK through the window.
>
> He climbs through the window.
>
> He scans the room.
>
> Above the desk is a wall with large computer monitors with multiple images of people Judas watches.
>
> He bolts for the desk and searches through the drawers. He looks around the room then sits at the computer.

After reading the first part of scene 39, it is evident that Matthew feels that the only way he can identify the Keystroke Killer and reveal the truth about him is to break into his lair. To write this aspect into the synopsis I must summarize the intent and action of the resolution from Matthew's perspective.

Let's consider alternative resolutions statements identified below.

Statement 1 – Resolution Statement

After Blaze ran from Matthew, he is more determined to reveal the truth about the Keystroke Killer. He breaks into Judas' lair and hacks into his computer. The truth is more revealing than Matthew could ever imagine.

Statement 2 – Resolution Statement

Later that day, Matthew breaks into Judas' home. He goes over to the computer and begins to search it.

Statement 3 – Resolution Statement

Distraught by Blaze's rejection, Matthew has one choice – to investigate Judas. He breaks into his home and discovers the shocking contents displayed on the computer monitor.

For the purpose of the synopsis, I choose the best resolution statement that maintains the tone and theme of *The Keystroke Killer* looking for one that is succinct and offers the most information. For me, all three of the statements meet these requirements. Therefore, I'll choose the shortest to save page space – statement 2. Remember that when writing the synopsis, being succinct is the key to effectiveness.

Working Synopsis with Resolution Statement Added

What would you do if the one person you loved most were erased from existence? MATTHEW, a grief stricken New York detective, lives this nightmare as he races to save BLAZE, the next victim, from the KEYSTROKE KILLER.

Matthew grieves the only way he knows – praying for his dead sister at the park where they spent time growing up as children. It is the same park Blaze, a young college student, finds peace and solitude as she feeds ducks in the pond. As children play under their mother's careful watch, JUDAS, aka the Keystroke Killer, lurks in the morning mist. It's a beautiful carefree day until TRACY, a small child, vanishes. The MOTHER screams which catches the attention of Blaze. Moments later, the child emerges from the bathroom. Relief overtakes Blaze, which soon turns to concern. She looks towards Judas. Only his smoking cigarette remains as Blaze feels as if someone watches her.

The sun rises as Blaze jogs along the park path. Meanwhile, Matthew, won't stop until he finds the person who killed his sister. Several young girls have gone missing, from a near-by park so Matthew starts his investigation there. He sees Blaze, who has an uncanny resemblance to his deceased sister. Matthew approaches Blaze. He warns her about the serial killer and suggests she shouldn't jog alone. Blaze pushes past Matthew. Judas looms in the morning fog.

That afternoon, Blaze meets her friends MAG and JENNI in a WI-FI café to work on a school project. When the subject of the Keystroke Killer emerges, Blaze shares her earlier encounter in the park with a stranger. This raises the curiosity between the girls just as Matthew, enters. Judas watches the interaction from afar. Blaze is uneasy about Matthew's entrance and leaves.

Later that night, Blaze prepares for bed by sipping a glass of red wine, followed by a nice hot shower to relax her. Matthew's uneasy causes him to guard Blaze's apartment from the outside. Grief overwhelms him as he looks at a picture of his sister he carries in his wallet. Judas watches them both from afar as the night turns to morning.

The next day, during Blaze's morning jog, Matthew confronts her again about the Keystroke Killer. Blaze's frustration grows with Matthew's insistence as she discards his warning. To gain her attention and trust, Matthew tells Blaze his sister was a victim of the Keystroke Killer, murdered by him less than three months ago; and she looks just like her escalating the tension between them. Judas watches from afar, as Blaze runs away from Matthew.

Judas keeps a close watch from afar on the conversation between Matthew and Blaze. Meanwhile, Mag and Jenni wait for Blaze at the WI-FI café.

Judas presses the "Delete" key on the keyboard as Mag, who leaves the WI-FI café dissolves into thin air. There is no trace of her. Judas leaves to a non-disclosed location. Shortly after, Blaze's cell phone rings.

Moments later, Matthew is more determined to rescue Blaze than before. After Blaze receives a phone call from Jenni telling her Mag has vanished, panic overcomes her leaving Matthew to expose the truth about an unknown reality of the world created by the Keystroke Killer. Nothing will convince Blaze as she pushes past Matthew.

Later that day, Matthew breaks into Judas' home. He goes over to the computer and begins to search it.

CHAPTER 14

DARK MOMENT

"A story to me means a plot where there is some surprise. Because that is how life is – full of surprises." Isaac Bashevis Singer – 1978 Nobel Prize in Literature Winner

NO WAY OUT

Just when you think that our protagonist has accomplished his task and defeated the antagonist, another shift in the plot transpires. Like the famous saying, "It's not over until the fat lady sings," the same applies to writing our synopsis. Audiences don't want to be robbed of victory. Remember, the audience is the mediator. If our protagonist achieves victory too suddenly, audiences feel cheated. If you delay too long, they become bored. As a screenwriter, you have to figure out the exact moment to give the protagonist another problem to solve. It is what I consider the "Dark Moment," with no way out. It is that moment where our protagonist feels he has won, then all of sudden, the world crashes around him. The monster, the mother always says doesn't exist, comes out from under the bed. Our hero rescues the girl; and shoots the villain only to discover the villain isn't dead and recaptures the girl and the hero. With the bomb ticking down, there is no way to escape. Everyone is about to die. The asteroid destroyed just in time only for the NASA scientist to discover a larger one coming toward earth that is bigger than the one they destroyed with no weapons left.

A good screenwriter can control the audience's emotion and create drama when and where he exactly wants it to occur. A great screenwriter will take the audience on the emotional roller coaster. The audience isn't in control. They are the neutral party mediator. The screenwriter has the power to manipulate our emotions.

The screenwriter uses Act I to allow the audience to get to know the characters. We'll either love or hate someone by the time the screenwriter develops the characters. We will identify with them or want to get as far away from them as possible. Then, before we know it, an inciting event occurs which sustains our emotions and drives us toward the main character.

The hardest section to write for a screenwriter is Act II. He or she has to convince the audience that the characters created are worth caring for or worth hating. The screenwriter wants us as an audience to give a damn about what is happening. Then, there is trouble. Enough trouble that as an audience we want the characters rescued and taken to safety.

Act III brings the audience along in the journey with you as the screenwriter. Just when we think there is no way out, our protagonist tries to overcome the impossible. Our hero dismantles the bomb only to discover it was the decoy and the real one is at the train station with only minutes to find it and to defuse it. I like to call this scenario the "Ticking Time Bomb" because it is a "No win" situation.

Screenwriters use a "No win" scenario to develop the next section of a synopsis. Our main character faces an insurmountable obstacle. There is no way out and the time bomb countdown is active. The antagonist puts the protagonist in jeopardy.

Therefore, when dissecting *The Keystroke Killer*, we look for the scene where the impossible "No win" scenario occurs. Looking closely at T*he Keystroke Killer*, it is evident this transition in the plot occurs in the end of Scene 39 when Matthew views Judas' computer as Blaze lays on the couch covered in blood with a knife in her hand. Look at the end of the scene.

Example 1 – Scene 39 Part from *The Keystroke Killer*

> He moves the mouse and the computer screen on the desk lights up. Most prominent in view is Jen.
>
> The monitor, left of Jen; that has been off, powers on.
>
> INSERT COMPUTER SCREEN:
>
> Blaze lays on her couch eyes wide-open. She is barely alive.
>
> Her white top with blood splatter barely covers her breasts.
>
> Blood oozes from several stab wounds. The long bladed knife with fresh blood lies in her lap.
>
> She tries to focus on the room that is blurry.
>
> BLAZE
> (faint whisper)
> Please forgive me.

This is the darkest moment for Matthew so far in the screenplay. Throughout the entire screenplay's timeline, Matthew has been on a quest to prevent the Keystroke Killer from killing Blaze. He vowed to avenge his sister's death. If he doesn't save Blaze, in his mind, he not only fails himself he also fails his sister. This is a powerful motivator for him to succeed. Failure is not an option.

Now, things look bleak for Matthew. He broke into the lair to discover Blaze's body covered in blood. He doesn't know if she is dead or alive. How do you think this impacts Matthew's mind? How would it influence yours? Furthermore, the screenplay never reveals the scene on how Blaze was injured or who was responsible for the injury. We only see Matthew's reaction. Therefore, to add the dark moment to the synopsis we will have to summarize the end of scene 39.

Statement 1 – Dark Moment

Precisely as Matthew turns on Judas' computer, an image of Blaze, covered in blood splatter, emerges on the screen. A blood stained knife lies in her lap. The once determined Matthew shows fear. He has failed.

Statement 2 – Dark Moment

A determined Matthew races to save Blaze from the Keystroke Killer. After breaking into his apartment, he turns on Judas' computer only to discover the image of Blaze's bloody body. It is as if he sees a ghost from his past. The knife, once used for protection, lays covered with blood in her lap. Wanting to escape from the view, he presses the "Delete" button. Blaze disappears.

Statement 3 – Dark Moment

The image of Blaze, covered in blood splatter, and a long bladed knife in her lap, pops up on the computer monitor. Matthew is horrified as if he sees a ghost from his past. He turns off the computer by pressing the "Delete" key on the keyboard. Blaze vanishes.

One of these dark moment statements are perfect for the synopsis. The statement chosen is determined by the one most prevalent and that captures the darkest moment for Matthew, our protagonist. I choose statement 3 as it is the most succinct. Look at it added to the working synopsis below.

Working Synopsis with Dark Moment Statement Added

What would you do if the one person you loved most were erased from existence? MATTHEW, a grief stricken New York detective, lives this nightmare as he races to save BLAZE, the next victim, from the KEYSTROKE KILLER.

Matthew grieves the only way he knows – praying for his dead sister at the park where they spent time growing up as children. It is the same park Blaze, a young college student, finds peace and solitude as she feeds ducks in the pond. As children play under their mother's careful watch, JUDAS, aka the Keystroke Killer, lurks in the morning mist. It's a beautiful carefree day until TRACY, a small child, vanishes. The MOTHER screams which catches the attention of Blaze. Moments later, the child emerges from the bathroom. Relief overtakes Blaze, which soon turns to concern. She looks towards Judas. Only his smoking cigarette remains as Blaze feels as if someone watches her.

The sun rises as Blaze jogs along the park path. Meanwhile, Matthew, won't stop until he finds the person who killed his sister. Several young girls have gone missing, from a near-by park so Matthew starts his investigation there.   He sees Blaze, who has an uncanny resemblance to his deceased sister.   Matthew approaches Blaze.   He warns her about the serial killer and suggests she shouldn't jog alone.   Blaze pushes past Matthew.   Judas looms in the morning fog.

That afternoon, Blaze meets her friends MAG and JENNI in a WI-FI café to work on a school project.   When the subject of the Keystroke Killer emerges, Blaze shares her earlier encounter in the park with a stranger.   This raises the curiosity between the girls just as Matthew, enters.   Judas watches the interaction from afar.   Blaze is uneasy about Matthew's entrance and leaves.

Later that night, Blaze prepares for bed by sipping a glass of red wine, followed by a nice hot shower to relax her.   Matthew's uneasy causes him to guard Blaze's apartment from the outside.   Grief overwhelms him as he looks at a picture of his sister he carries in his wallet. Judas watches them both from afar as the night turns to morning.

The next day, during Blaze's morning jog, Matthew confronts her again about the Keystroke Killer.   Blaze's frustration grows with Matthew's insistence as she discards his warning.   To gain her attention and trust, Matthew tells Blaze his sister was a victim of the Keystroke Killer, murdered by him less than three months ago; and she looks just like her escalating the tension between them.   Judas watches from afar, as Blaze runs away from Matthew.

Judas keeps a close watch from afar on the conversation between Matthew and Blaze. Meanwhile, Mag and Jenni wait for Blaze at the WI-FI café.

Judas presses the "Delete" key on the keyboard as Mag, who leaves the WI-FI café dissolves into thin air.   There is no trace of her.   Judas leaves to a non-disclosed location.   Shortly after, Blaze's cell phone rings.

Moments later, Matthew is more determined to rescue Blaze than before.   After Blaze receives a phone call from Jenni, telling her Mag has vanished; panic overcomes her leaving Matthew to expose the truth about an unknown reality of the world created by the Keystroke Killer.   Nothing will convince Blaze as she pushes past Matthew.

Later that day, Matthew breaks into Judas' home.   He goes over to the computer and begins to search it.

The image of Blaze, covered in blood splatter, and a long bladed knife in her lap, pops up on the computer monitor.   Matthew is horrified as if he sees a ghost from his past.   He turns off the computer by pressing the "Delete" key on the keyboard.   Blaze vanishes.

Matthew pressing the delete key.

CHAPTER 15

FILLED WITH ANTICIPATION

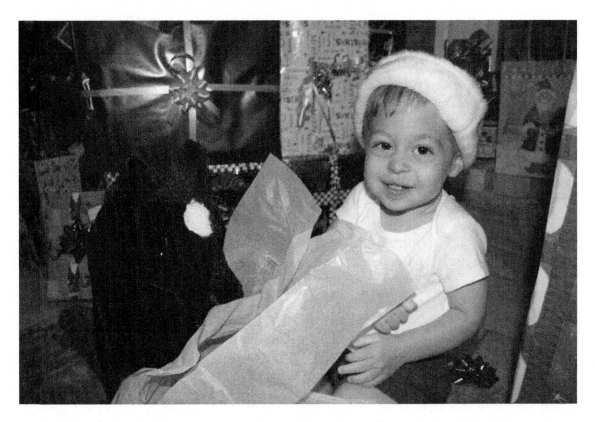

"As much as most of the actors were kind of curious to know what their character meant in relation to the script and to the plot, they really were quite happy to be part of the adventure of not knowing." Radha Mitchell – Australian Actress – best known for *Finding Neverland*

MAKE THEM WAIT

When I think of the word anticipation two things cross my mind: Christmas and Heinz ketchup. They both have one thing in common – they make you wait. No matter how much of a hurry you are in, you can't rush Christmas morning and you can't rush Heinz ketchup.

This year I enjoyed a special moment with my youngest grandson. He is 18 months old and is just now getting into everything Christmas. I was babysitting him the day I put up my Christmas tree. His eyes were wide-open as I turned on the lights. He didn't know what all of this meant, but he knew it meant something.

As we worked together carefully placing decorations on the tree, I realized how filled with anticipation he was each time I brought out a new ornament. He didn't care about the shape, size, or color. The only thing that mattered to him at this moment was how each ornament filled him with anticipation. I'll never forget how he gasped with joy each time I brought out a new one and he was able to place it on the Christmas tree. His eyes lit up and the smile on his face was pure joy. His joyful innocence; and anticipation is exactly what I need to remember when approaching the next section of the synopsis.

Instead of revealing everything at once, as screenwriters we need to make our audience wait in anticipation. As slow as Heinz ketchup is to pour from the bottle, it's worth it when you dip hot fries into them – your mouth begins to water as you are filled with anticipation for the first bite. Remembering how you feel when you anticipate something is a key factor when writing a screenplay and the section in relationship to the synopsis. Anticipation is that important. Let's discuss ways in which a screenwriter can create anticipation in their script.

SLOW DOWN YOU MOVE TO FAST

The song *The 59th Street Bridge Song,* in the late sixties, also called, *Feelin Groovy*, performed by the magnificent duo Simon and Garfunkel, says it best, "Slow down, you move too fast. You've got to make the morning last." I feel about the anticipation section for any synopsis that way. You don't want it to be less than "Groovy." If you move to fast toward your ending, it is very disappointing for your audience. They feel cheated and let down. If everything the

protagonist does is for naught by going too fast, you lose your audience's attention.

I call this method to create anticipation the "Groovy Theory." By this, I mean at one point in Act II, you have to slow things down a bit. If things have been dramatic, you might want to put in a moment to stop and smell the roses. Don't make it look obvious and while there, don't keep your audience there too long. It's a balancing act at best.

The Snail Theory

The "Snail Theory" is when a screenwriter carefully designs plot points that make your audience wait in anticipation. Create the moment in which your audience takes a long deep breath not knowing what your protagonist is going to do next or what your antagonist is going to throw their way. This is a good moment to tie in any supporting characters and their confusion with the world. Don't waste your  audience's time with confusing plot points. Make each plot and sub plot count. Maximize your opportunities. Also, make certain that the resolution matches the seriousness of the plot. Don't throw in a comedic resolution for a serious moment. This too serves as a catalyst for confusion. Match your momentum with the momentum of your characters. Slow things down and make your audience wait.

To apply this theory to our developing synopsis, we have to write it in. By referring to the beat sheet, you can identify the momentum in your screenplay where to slow it down.

At the last point in developing the synopsis for *The Keystroke Killer*, from the beat sheet, we know that our protagonist has just lived his darkest moment – Matthew found Blaze dead. To slow things down and make sure I build in anticipation, I had to plan for the "Snail Theory." A quick response would be for Matthew to turn to anger, destroy Judas' apartment or go on a rampage. To do so, wouldn't be slowing things down. Would it? This scenario is expected by the audience.

How many times have you watched a movie and immediately following the darkest moment, the protagonist goes on a rampage. A rampage isn't slowing things down. I dare to be different. Therefore, I build in anticipation.

First, I have Matthew sitting in grief and shock after just seeing Blaze covered in blood. Remember at this moment, it is also an internal conflict for Matthew. He has failed to avenge his sister's death and now has a second failure by not having kept Blaze safe. How much more of an emotional roller coaster will Matthew be able to handle? He's at a point of no return. Instead of going into a violent rampage, he pulls out the picture of his sister and reflects on her. It's the "Snail Theory" in action. I don't wait too long to ruin the progression of the plot. His reflection turns to anger transferring all emotions when he pulls his gun from his holster and shoots the computer monitor. The emotional roller coaster is fulfilled in the plot.

The key to this pivotal plot point is that Matthew's rampage wasn't immediate. After the rampage of destroying the computer, Matthew rushes from Judas' lair. If you are questioning how Matthew knew to go to the lair in the first place, this information is in the pilot episode *Transcendence*. Again, I apply my anticipation theory by not moving too fast. As the screenwriter, I don't explain or show to the audience where he is heading. I make the audience wait in anticipation to find out. It could be a number of places. Look at scene 40 to view how I wrote this into *The Keystroke Killer*. The scene begins with Matthew having just seeing Blaze covered in blood on the computer monitor. I pick up from that point to build in the anticipation of what will happen next.

Example – Scene 40 from *The Keystroke Killer*

40. INT. THE KEYSTROKE KILLER LAIR - DAY

Matthew sits with a blank stare as if he sees a ghost. His left-hand rests on the keyboard and the right-hand controls the mouse.

INSERT: Matthew's right pointer finger as he presses THE DELETE key.

The screen with the image of Blaze goes blank. STATIC NOISE.

Matthew pulls his gun from his holster.

He SHOOTS the computer screen.

Matthew rushes out of the lair. He is angry beyond belief.

Once Matthew views Blaze's bloody body, he presses the "Delete" button and the screen goes black followed by static noise. This is the same scenario as when Judas pressed the "Delete" key making Mag vanish. These two actions combined inform the audience how the Keystroke Killer murders his victims. We first see it in the death of Mag as a foreshadowing tool, then it is confirmed by Matthew, when he accidently "Deletes" Blaze. However, do we really know who injured Blaze? It isn't ever clearly stated. The audience has to surmise it. However, the answer to who injures Blaze isn't ever clearly stated until the pilot television script. There are facts that lead to the answer.

- We know young girls are killed in a park.
- We know that Judas watches everyone.
- We know that Judas pressed the "Delete" button and made Mag vanish.
- We know that Judas left is lair after viewing the conversation between Matthew and Blaze.
- We know Matthew was mad at Blaze for not believing him.
- We know that Matthew went to Judas' lair and turned on the computer.
- We know that Matthew saw Blaze covered in blood with the knife in her lap.
- We know that Matthew pressed the "Delete" button while in Judas' apartment.
- We know that Matthew went to Blaze's apartment after her death.
- We know that the Landlord told Matthew that Blaze's apartment had been vacant for more than a year.
- We know Judas called Matthew at Blaze's apartment and told him she never existed.

That's how you build anticipation. When a screenwriter doesn't state the obvious and leave things for the audience to interpret, it builds anticipation. To add the anticipation statement for a developing synopsis, write a single sentence that is open-ended. By open-ended, I mean that the sentence could lead to any outcome and it is not stated.

Look at the following options for the anticipation statement for the synopsis.

Statement 1 – Building Anticipation

The view is overwhelming to Matthew. He leaves Judas' apartment.

Statement 2 – Building Anticipation

After looking at a picture of his sister, in anger, he pulls out his gun from his holster and shoots the computer screen. Matthew heads out for revenge.

Statement 3 – Building Anticipation

Matthew rushes from Judas' home.

All three statements are appropriate for the synopsis. Since the plot development ties to an emotion, I believe either statement 1 or 2 would best serve the purpose for the synopsis. I'll choose statement 2 because it describes the entire scene that builds on the "Snail Theory." Here is the working synopsis with the anticipation statement included.

Working Synopsis with Anticipation Statement Added

What would you do if the one person you loved most were erased from existence? MATTHEW, a grief stricken New York detective, lives this nightmare as he races to save BLAZE, the next victim, from the KEYSTROKE KILLER.

Matthew grieves the only way he knows – praying for his dead sister at the park where they spent time growing up as children. It is the same park Blaze, a young college student, finds peace and solitude as she feeds ducks in the pond. As children play under their mother's careful watch, JUDAS, aka the Keystroke Killer, lurks in the morning mist. It's a beautiful carefree day until TRACY, a small child, vanishes. The MOTHER screams which catches the attention of Blaze. Moments later, the child emerges from the bathroom. Relief overtakes Blaze, which soon turns to concern. She looks towards Judas. Only his smoking cigarette remains as Blaze feels as if someone watches her.

The sun rises as Blaze jogs along the park path. Meanwhile, Matthew, won't stop until he finds the person who killed his sister. Several young girls have gone missing, from a near-by park so Matthew starts his investigation there. He sees Blaze, who has an uncanny resemblance to his deceased sister. Matthew approaches Blaze. He warns her about the serial killer and suggests she shouldn't jog alone. Blaze pushes past Matthew. Judas looms in the morning fog.

That afternoon, Blaze meets her friends MAG and JENNI in a WI-FI café to work on a school project. When the subject of the Keystroke Killer emerges, Blaze shares her earlier encounter in the park with a stranger. This raises the curiosity between the girls just as

Matthew, enters. Judas watches the interaction from afar. Blaze is uneasy about Matthew's entrance and leaves.

Later that night, Blaze prepares for bed by sipping a glass of red wine, followed by a nice hot shower to relax her. Matthew's uneasy causes him to guard Blaze's apartment from the outside. Grief overwhelms him as he looks at a picture of his sister he carries in his wallet. Judas watches them both from afar as the night turns to morning.

The next day, during Blaze's morning jog, Matthew confronts her again about the Keystroke Killer. Blaze's frustration grows with Matthew's insistence as she discards his warning. To gain her attention and trust, Matthew tells Blaze his sister was a victim of the Keystroke Killer, murdered by him less than three months ago; and she looks just like her escalating the tension between them. Judas watches from afar, as Blaze runs away from Matthew.

Judas keeps a close watch from afar on the conversation between Matthew and Blaze. Meanwhile, Mag and Jenni wait for Blaze at the WI-FI café.

Judas presses the "Delete" key on the keyboard as Mag, who leaves the WI-FI café dissolves into thin air. There is no trace of her. Judas leaves to a non-disclosed location. Shortly after, Blaze's cell phone rings.

Moments later, Matthew is more determined to rescue Blaze than before. After Blaze receives a phone call from Jenni, telling her Mag has vanished; panic overcomes her leaving Matthew to expose the truth about an unknown reality of the world created by the Keystroke Killer. Nothing will convince Blaze as she pushes past Matthew.

Later that day, Matthew breaks into Judas' home. He goes over to the computer and begins to search it.

The image of Blaze, covered in blood splatter, and a long bladed knife in her lap, pops up on the computer monitor. Matthew is horrified as if he sees a ghost from his past. He turns off the computer by pressing the "Delete" key on the keyboard. Blaze vanishes.

After looking at a picture of his sister, in anger, he pulls out his gun from his holster and shoots the computer screen. Matthew heads out for revenge.

Matthew fires at the computer monitor.

CHAPTER 16

REGAIN CONTROL

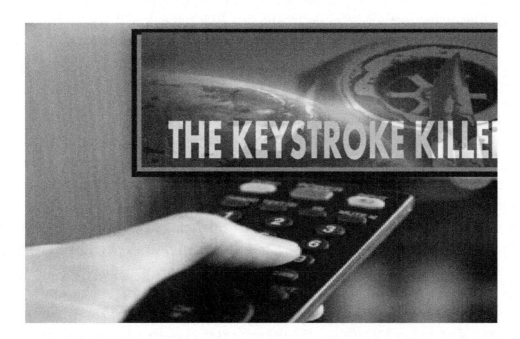

"This means keeping many trails open at once, inevitably requiring a fairly parallel plot. This plot should be discovered rather than announced, so show, don't tell." Graham Nelson – Creator of the Inform Design System for Interactive Fiction Games

REMOTE CONTROL

After reading *The Keystroke Killer*, it gives a new meaning to the words "remote control." We finish reading the screenplay knowing one individual – Judas, controls the world. He has the power to erase us from the face of the earth by pressing the "Delete" key on a keyboard.

During the last chapter, I wrote the anticipation section of the synopsis using the "Snail Theory." I make the audience wait prior to revealing the outcome and resolution to the plot. The plot and storyline aren't over yet. A well-written screenplay will provide another twist providing the protagonist the opportunity to regain control over the antagonist. I do the same thing in *The Keystroke Killer*. Matthew, determined to bring revenge on Judas, investigates Blaze's death. Ultimately as a detective, he wants to bring justice and put Judas away for a very long time. His motivation comes from his vow to avenge his sister's death. As the screenwriter, I don't think at this moment Matthew cares how he brings down Judas, just as long as he does. Motivated by the fact that Judas killed his sister, he wants the control. He has already failed in his own eyes. He believes Judas killed Blaze. Does this mean that the Keystroke Killer is in control? Does this look and feel that way to you?

To contend with this plot development as a screenwriter, Matthew has to regain control. By the mere fact he pulled his revolver and shot Judas' computer screen, to him he regained his control. However, plot wise, it isn't strong enough. I need a deeper catalyst for Matthew. For him, his very own survival and psyche are attached to the fact either he will defeat Judas or Judas will defeat him. It is the old-fashion good vs. evil plot twist. Matthew isn't the type of character to allow defeat. Is he? He's strong, determined, focused, bold, and witty. Therefore, he has only one choice – bring down the Keystroke Killer. This is the only way to avenge his sister's death and not be a failure in his own eyes. Failure will devastate Matthew. He has to be able to look into the mirror each day and like what he sees. At this moment in the screenplay, he can't face himself. He has to regain control one way or another.

The moment Matthew regains control is inferred rather than stated. It is intrinsic in design and not extrinsic. To him, it's a mind game he chooses to play with Judas. Matthew regains control when he learns something new that he hasn't known in the past. Look at scenes 41 and 42 from *The Keystroke Killer* that outlines this plot development.

Example 1 – Scene 41 from *The Keystroke Killer*

    41. INT. LIVING ROOM - DAY

        Blaze's apartment is clean and untouched.

        No evidence of blood or foul play.

        The door opens. Matthew and the LANDLORD enter.

> MATTHEW
> How long did you say the apartment
> has been vacant?

> LANDLORD
> For a year.

Matthew begins to pick things up from the coffee table and expect them.

He pulls a chair over to a vent and looks through it.

He searches for something specific to no avail. He goes from one item to the next throughout the apartment.

He stands in front of the vase. Some shines in the light.

He looks into the vase and retrieves a knife. He pulls the knife quickly out of the vase and puts it in his jacket unnoticed by the Landlord.

> MATTHEW
> What about the girl that lived here?   She was just here.
> Her name is Blaze.

> LANDLORD
> You must be mistaken. The last
> person to rent this apartment was
> an old widow. Ms. Cavalier I believe.
> She died over a year ago. No one wants to
> lie where a dead body was found.

Matthew's cell phone RINGS just as he finds a small hidden camera. He puts the camera in his pocket.

He answers the phone and continues to search.

> MATTHEW
> Detective Morrison. (beat). What
> do you mean Blaze Angela doesn't exist? I
> talked to her this morning.

42. INT. THE KEYSTROKE KILLER LAIR - DAY

Judas sits at his desk talking on the phone.

JUDAS
That's right detective. There is no such person.

THE POWER OF KNOWLEDGE

Although it looks like the Keystroke Killer has won, Matthew has learned valuable information from Judas. For the first time, Matthew learns people the Keystroke Killer is murdering not only die, but also erased by him from the face of the earth. There is no record of them ever living. It could be that at this moment in the plot development, Matthew realizes he is responsible for Blaze's death. It also provides him additional motive to bring Judas to justice. His control is from the power of knowledge where before, he based his power from the standpoint of revenge.

With that said, keep in mind that for a protagonist to regain control doesn't mean that he has to take over. That is predictable. As the screenwriter, you too can take control for the protagonist. Offering a different angle and method of control is powerful. There is nothing more powerful in the world than knowledge. Anytime your main character obtains knowledge, it is powerful. It allows the protagonist to regain control. The difference is what the protagonist does with the knowledge and newly found power.

The synopsis is now ready to include the section describing how the protagonist regains power. Look at the following statements that summarize scenes 41 and 42.

Statement 1 – Regaining Power

Blaze's apartment is empty. No trace of Blaze remains. Matthew, escorted by the Landlord enters the apartment just as he receives a phone call from Judas. During the conversation, Judas reveals to Matthew that there is no evidence to support the existence of Blaze.

Statement 2 – Regaining Power

As Matthew enters Blaze's empty apartment with the Landlord, he receives a phone call from Judas. There is no evidence that Blaze has ever occupied the apartment. The landlord confirms adding to the mystery.

Statement 3 – Regaining Power

Matthew arrives at Blaze's apartment escorted by the Landlord.   The apartment is blood free and there is no evidence to prove Blaze previously occupied the premises.   Judas calls Matthew and informs him there is no record Blaze's existence.

Logically, adding any of the above statements to the synopsis will capture the essence of scenes 41 and 42. Look at the working synopsis when I add statement 3.

Working Synopsis with Regaining Control Statement Added

What would you do if the one person you loved most were erased from existence? MATTHEW, a grief stricken New York detective, lives this nightmare as he races to save BLAZE, the next victim, from the KEYSTROKE KILLER.

Matthew grieves the only way he knows – praying for his dead sister at the park where they spent time growing up as children. It is the same park Blaze, a young college student, finds peace and solitude as she feeds ducks in the pond. As children play under their mother's careful watch, JUDAS, aka the Keystroke Killer, lurks in the morning mist. It's a beautiful carefree day until TRACY, a small child, vanishes. The MOTHER screams which catches the attention of Blaze. Moments later, the child emerges from the bathroom. Relief overtakes Blaze, which soon turns to concern. She looks towards Judas. Only his smoking cigarette remains as Blaze feels as if someone watches her.

The sun rises as Blaze jogs along the park path. Meanwhile, Matthew, won't stop until he finds the person who killed his sister. Several young girls have gone missing, from a near-by park so Matthew starts his investigation there.   He sees Blaze, who has an uncanny resemblance to his deceased sister. Matthew approaches Blaze. He warns her about the serial killer and suggests she shouldn't jog alone. Blaze pushes past Matthew. Judas looms in the morning fog.

That afternoon, Blaze meets her friends MAG and JENNI in a WI-FI café to work on a school project.   When the subject of the Keystroke Killer emerges, Blaze shares her earlier encounter in the park with a stranger. This raises the curiosity between the girls just as Matthew, enters. Judas watches the interaction from afar. Blaze is uneasy about Matthew's entrance and leaves.

Later that night, Blaze prepares for bed by sipping a glass of red wine, followed by a nice hot shower to relax her. Matthew's uneasy causes him to guard Blaze's apartment from the outside. Grief overwhelms him as he looks at a picture of his sister he carries in his wallet. Judas watches them both from afar as the night turns to morning.

The next day, during Blaze's morning jog, Matthew confronts her again about the Keystroke Killer. Blaze's frustration grows with Matthew's insistence as she discards his warning. To gain her attention and trust, Matthew tells Blaze his sister was a victim of the Keystroke

Killer, murdered by him less than three months ago; and she looks just like her escalating the tension between them. Judas watches from afar, as Blaze runs away from Matthew.

Judas keeps a close watch from afar on the conversation between Matthew and Blaze. Meanwhile, Mag and Jenni wait for Blaze at the WI-FI café.

Judas presses the "Delete" key on the keyboard as Mag, who leaves the WI-FI café dissolves into thin air. There is no trace of her. Judas leaves to a non-disclosed location. Shortly after, Blaze's cell phone rings.

Moments later, Matthew is more determined to rescue Blaze than before. After Blaze receives a phone call from Jenni, telling her Mag has vanished; panic overcomes her leaving Matthew to expose the truth about an unknown reality of the world created by the Keystroke Killer. Nothing will convince Blaze as she pushes past Matthew.

Later that day, Matthew breaks into Judas' home. He goes over to the computer and begins to search it.

The image of Blaze, covered in blood splatter, and a long bladed knife in her lap, pops up on the computer monitor. Matthew is horrified as if he sees a ghost from his past. He turns off the computer by pressing the "Delete" key on the keyboard. Blaze vanishes.

In anger, he pulls his gun from his holster and shoots the computer screen. Matthew heads out for revenge.

Matthew arrives at Blaze's apartment escorted by the Landlord. The apartment is blood free and there is no evidence to prove Blaze previously occupied the premises. Judas calls Matthew and informs him there is no record Blaze's existence.

CHAPTER 17

THE FINAL COUNTDOWN

"To this day, I get rewrite offers where they say, "We feel this script needs work with character, dialogue, plot, and tone," and when you ask what's left, they say, "Well, the typing is very good." – John Sayles – American Film Director and Screenwriter – *Jurassic Park IV*

PROBLEM SOLVED

When is it time to bring resolution to your plot? I say when the protagonist takes the very last breath, the last scene begins, or the very last word spoken. At this point, it's not about what has happened. It's all about the future and where you leave your audience.

It is my belief that the two most important parts of a screenplay are the beginning first 10 pages and the ending. If I had to choose between the two, I would vote for the ending of a screenplay because how it ends, is pivotal to the success of the film for an audience. Audiences either walk away from a film liking the ending or hating it. The way they talk about the ending will make others want to go see the movie or stay away from it. The same is true for the ending you write for the synopsis. It must leave the reader wanting to read the entire script. You have to consider three questions when developing your ending:

1. Has the plot been resolved?
2. Is there something left unsaid?
3. Have you tied up all of the loose ends?

If the answers to the above questions are "Yes," then it's time to announce and write the final resolution to bring your screenplay to a close. The answers also govern the style and type of ending you choose rather than your plot design. There are four common endings for screenplays used in Hollywood:

1. The Happy-ending
2. The Debbie Downer ending
3. The Bittersweet ending
4. The Cliffhanger ending

The Happy-Ending

Most audiences find screenplays with happy-endings the most fulfilling. Therefore,  screenplays with happy-endings are the most attractive to agents, managers, and producers. A happy-ending will put your protagonist in a good light with him or her winning. Consider the following examples.

• The bad guy taken down.
• The nerdy boy gets the sexy girl.
• Demons destroyed by the hero.

- The bumbling scientist saves the world by blowing up the asteroid at the last second.

All happy-endings leave the audience in a "feel good" mood.

The Debbie Downer Ending

Portrayed by Rachel Dratch on *Saturday Night Live,* Debbie Downer is a fictional character who constantly brings bad news and negative feelings to those around her. Nothing good ever happens. People are sad. A screenplay with a sad ending is a Debbie Downer ending. Most often, bad guys winning, the hero loses and is defeated characterize screenplays falling into this category. These screenplays aren't that popular, but do have audience appeal. A Debbie Downer ending leaves the audience feeling let down. They shake their heads in dismay.

The Bittersweet Ending

When someone begins a conversation by saying, "I have good news and bad news," you know there is going to hear something good and something bad. The bittersweet ending for a screenplay is just like hearing goods news and bad news at

the same time. Although our protagonist wins in the end, he or she loses something along the way. A good example is a homeless man winning the lottery only to discover he is has one month to live. There is always a "cost" to the protagonist. A bittersweet ending leaves the audience with mixed emotions.

The Cliffhanger Ending

When a screenplay ends and you are uncertain as to how your protagonist will go from that point forward is a cliffhanger ending. The resolution can go any direction and in order to find out what happens you have to wait and watch the sequel or next episode.

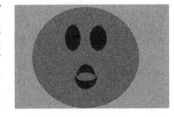

A cliffhanger ending leaves the audience wanting to know the outcome so they come back for more. They have a high emotional connection with the outcome and go to great lengths to find it out. This is what makes sequels popular.

WRITING THE RESOLUTION SECTION

When writing the resolution section for the synopsis, I begin by identifying the type of ending for the screenplay. This directs your resolution section by keeping it in alignment with the style and tone of your screenplay. Your resolution also strongly relates to your genre. For instance, a romantic comedy usually has a happy-ending. An action packed feature drama typically equates to a cliffhanger, whereas, a sci-fi can lean toward many directions. To write the synopsis resolution section for *The Keystroke Killer*, I first located the point in the screenplay that resonates with the resolution. This point can also easily identified by referring to the beat sheet.

Rereading the final scene and ending of the screenplay, I determine the resolution is located in scene 43 and falls within the category of a bittersweet ending. The reasons are clear. First, Matthew, our protagonist, is able to identify where the Keystroke Killer lives. He broke in and destroyed his equipment. He was close to capturing Judas. However, in Matthew's eyes he failed. He wasn't able to keep the vow he made to his sister and he saw Blaze injured. He assumes she is dead when he sees her. He has no idea, that it is his action by pressing the "Delete" key that killed her.

To deal with Blaze's death and bring resolution to the screenplay, Matthew returns to the park where he first saw Blaze. In remembrance of her death, he places a long-stemmed pink rose on the park bench where he waited for her each morning. In the opening scene, Matthew threw a rose into the pond at the park and prayed for his sister. This is Matthew's way of coping. It also brings the audience on the emotional ride with him. The rose signifies the blood stains of his sister and now Blaze at the hands of the Keystroke Killer.

Look at the scene.

Example – Scene 43 from *The Keystroke Killer*

> 43. EXT. PARK - SUNSET
>
>> Matthew, distraught from the day's events, walks along the jogging path. He carries a long-stemmed pink rose.
>>
>> He places it on the park bench where he first sat and waited for Blaze.
>>
>> The sun sets over the park.

To add this to the synopsis requires me to summarize the action description. Since the action description for this scene is short, it almost suffices without rewording it. Nevertheless, I will take a shot at it to see if it improves. I always like to have options when writing essential areas of the synopsis.

Statement 1 – Resolution

> Saddened by the death of Blaze, Matthew remembers her death by placing a pink long-stemmed rose on the park bench where they first met.

Statement 2 – Resolution

> Grief overpowers Matthew as he reflects on Blaze's death. He returns to the park and places a long-stemmed pink rose on the park bench. He silently vows to take down the Keystroke Killer.

Statement 3 – Resolution

> Matthew, distraught from the day's events, walks along the jogging path where he first met Blaze. He carries a long-stemmed pink rose and places it on the park bench vowing to avenge her death.

Essentially, all three statements say the same thing. It is a matter of determining which one flows with the rest of the synopsis, while capturing the resolution and the essence of the screenplay.

Below, is the working synopsis.

Working Synopsis with Resolution Statement Added

What would you do if the one person you loved most were erased from existence? MATTHEW, a grief stricken New York detective, lives this nightmare as he races to save BLAZE, the next victim, from the KEYSTROKE KILLER.

Matthew grieves the only way he knows – praying for his dead sister at the park where they spent time growing up as children. It is the same park Blaze, a young college student, finds peace and solitude as she feeds ducks in the pond. As children play under their mother's careful watch, JUDAS, aka the Keystroke Killer, lurks in the morning mist. It's a beautiful carefree day until TRACY, a small child, vanishes. The MOTHER screams which catches the attention of Blaze. Moments later, the child emerges from the bathroom. Relief overtakes Blaze, which soon turns to concern. She looks towards Judas. Only his smoking cigarette remains as Blaze feels as if someone watches her.

The sun rises as Blaze jogs along the park path. Meanwhile, Matthew, won't stop until he finds the person who killed his sister. Several young girls have gone missing, from a near-by park so Matthew starts his investigation there. He sees Blaze, who has an uncanny resemblance to his deceased sister. Matthew approaches Blaze. He warns her about the serial killer and suggests she shouldn't jog alone. Blaze pushes past Matthew. Judas looms in the morning fog.

That afternoon, Blaze meets her friends MAG and JENNI in a WI-FI café to work on a school project. When the subject of the Keystroke Killer emerges, Blaze shares her earlier encounter in the park with a stranger. This raises the curiosity between the girls just as Matthew, enters. Judas watches the interaction from afar. Blaze is uneasy about Matthew's entrance and leaves.

Later that night, Blaze prepares for bed by sipping a glass of red wine, followed by a nice hot shower to relax her. Matthew's uneasy causes him to guard Blaze's apartment from the outside. Grief overwhelms him as he looks at a picture of his sister he carries in his wallet. Judas watches them both from afar as the night turns to morning.

The next day, during Blaze's morning jog, Matthew confronts her again about the Keystroke Killer. Blaze's frustration grows with Matthew's insistence as she discards his warning. To gain her attention and trust, Matthew tells Blaze his sister was a victim of the Keystroke Killer, murdered by him less than three months ago; and she looks just like her escalating the tension between them. Judas watches from afar, as Blaze runs away from Matthew.

Judas keeps a close watch from afar on the conversation between Matthew and Blaze. Meanwhile, Mag and Jenni wait for Blaze at the WI-FI café.

Judas presses the "Delete" key on the keyboard as Mag, who leaves the WI-FI café dissolves into thin air. There is no trace of her. Judas leaves to a non-disclosed location. Shortly after, Blaze's cell phone rings.

Moments later, Matthew is more determined to rescue Blaze than before. After Blaze receives a phone call from Jenni, telling her Mag has vanished; panic overcomes her leaving Matthew to expose the truth about an unknown reality of the world created by the Keystroke Killer. Nothing will convince Blaze as she pushes past Matthew.

Later that day, Matthew breaks into Judas' home. He goes over to the computer and begins to search it.

The image of Blaze, covered in blood splatter, and a long bladed knife in her lap, pops up on the computer monitor. Matthew is horrified as if he sees a ghost from his past. He turns off the computer by pressing the "Delete" key on the keyboard. Blaze vanishes.

In anger, he pulls his gun from his holster and shoots the computer screen. Matthew heads out for revenge.

Matthew arrives at Blaze's apartment escorted by the Landlord. The apartment is blood free and there is no evidence to prove Blaze previously occupied the premises. Judas calls Matthew and informs him there is no record Blaze's existence.

Matthew, distraught from the day's events, walks along the jogging path where he first met Blaze. He carries a long-stemmed pink rose and places it on the park bench vowing to avenge her death.

CHAPTER 18

HAPPILY EVER AFTER

"I just want to live happily ever after, every now and then." Jimmy Buffett –
Musician and Actor

DON'T STEAL THE THUNDER

It's important for all screenwriters to remember that not every storyline has to have
a happy-ending. There are many options to choose when developing your ending.
For example, in *The Keystroke Killer*, it's not necessary for Matthew to fall in love
with Blaze. Likewise, it's not necessary for him to save her. Matthew may decide
that he has to come to grip with the fact he couldn't save his sister who now haunts
and dictates his every move.

Matthew may decide that he has to search within his soul to find meaning in his
everyday life. Having alternate endings have value in marketing a DVD.

Whatever the ending and resolution may become, the ending you choose must be
memorable. If the audience doesn't remember your ending, doesn't think about it,

and it doesn't haunt them, then it's probably not a good ending. As for *The Keystroke Killer*, Matthew has to be in charge. We know and understand this. In the end, he has to take control of an uncontrollable situation.

If Matthew catches the Keystroke Killer or another detective comes in at the last minute and resolves the case, where's the satisfaction for the audience? All of danger he and Blaze faced would be for naught. As a screenwriter, you don't want to fall into the "Mick Jagger" trap. The iconic *Rolling Stones* lyrics, "I can't get no, satisfaction," isn't what you want your audience to experience. I can safely say if Matthew has the fortitude to be our main character, then he deserves to be the one who brings resolution to the
plot. This is one lesson that screenwriters must learn. Don't steal the thunder from your protagonist.

Giving power and not taking the thunder away from the protagonist must be evident in your synopsis too. It doesn't come free or easy. There is a give and take as the plot develops. Just make sure that in the end the protagonist has the last word. I don't mean this literally in dialogue. Sometimes, silence or a disappearance is the last word.

Look at scene 44 ending the screenplay. It brings final resolution and gives Matthew the last word. He evolved from the beginning of the screenplay where grief drove him. In the end, revenge motivates him. He focuses on Blaze's death in order to bring justice. He has to find a way to overcome his previous failure. Again, that is the only way he will be able to look at himself in the mirror. A person's reflection in a mirror is a powerful thing for individuals to reflect on their actions and current situations.

If Matthew were standing in front of the mirror, what do you think would be going through his mind?

What would go through your mind if you were in the same situation and failed to achieve a promise you made to your sister?

It's the same feeling for Matthew and he will find resolution.

In *The Keystroke Killer*, Matthew challenges Judas and takes total control of the situation. The ending transforms from bittersweet to a cliffhanger, which sets up for either a sequel to a film or a television series. In essence, this short screenplay is a pilot script for a feature film that introduces the television series *The Keystroke Killer.* I created which follows Matthew as he attempts to reveal the identity and capture the Keystroke Killer. Each episode builds on the context as Matthew faces new challenges and solves murders.

Example – Ending from *The Keystroke Killer*

44. EXT. THE KEYSTROKE KILLER LAIR– NIGHT

Matthew walks up to the Judas' lair and stands guard. If looks could kill, Judas would be dead. Matthew pulls out his wallet and looks at the picture of his sister.

MATTHEW
This is far from over.

GUN SHOT.

FADE TO BLACK

To incorporate the cliffhanger ending into the synopsis is to summarize the final event. You want the final sentence in your synopsis to have power over your audience so that they insist on reading the screenplay. If you give everything away, then there isn't a reason for them to read the screenplay. If you don't provide enough information, then the reader questions your ability as a screenwriter. Draw the line by writing a tantalizing ending statement that leaves the reader with a final image to embrace and embed in his or her memory forever. After reading the final statement, you want them not to be able to get the final image out of their head. If you succeed, your synopsis is worthy of landing you a deal.

Listed below are several options to end *The Keystroke Killer* synopsis with a powerful image.

Statement 1 - Final Image

Matthews stands guard outside the lair. He catches a glimpse of Judas through the window. After looking at the picture of his sister, Matthew fires his gun. He vows to avenge his sister's death.

Statement 2 - Final Image

That night, Matthew stands guard outside the Keystroke Killer's lair. He wants revenge at all cost. He pulls his sister's picture from his wallet. Matthew vows to avenge her death. He pulls out his gun, GUNSHOT.

Statement 3 – Final Image

That night, Matthew stands guard outside the Keystroke Killer's lair. The one man who watches others – Matthew now watches. Pulling out from his wallet his sister's picture, Matthew vows to avenge her death. He retrieves his gun. GUNSHOT. Nothing but blackness and silence remains.

Statement 4 – Final Image

Under dimly lit streetlights, Matthew stands guard below the lair. Revenge is prominent across his face. He pulls a picture of his sister from his wallet. When Judas crosses the window, Matthew pulls out his gun and fires. Blackness surrounds the mist floating up toward the lights. Then there is darkness and silence.

Without looking ahead at the statement I include into my synopsis, which one do you think I chose? Which one presents a final image in your mind? Now I'll add the final image statement I think is the most impactful to the working synopsis for *The Keystroke Killer*.

Working Synopsis with Resolution Statement Added

What would you do if the one person you loved most were erased from existence? MATTHEW, a grief stricken New York detective, lives this nightmare as he races to save BLAZE, the next victim, from the KEYSTROKE KILLER.

Matthew grieves the only way he knows – praying for his dead sister at the park where they spent time growing up as children. It is the same park Blaze, a young college student, finds peace and solitude as she feeds ducks in the pond. As children play under their mother's careful watch, JUDAS, aka the Keystroke Killer, lurks in the morning mist. It's a beautiful carefree day until TRACY, a small child, vanishes. The MOTHER screams which catches the attention of Blaze. Moments later, the child emerges from the bathroom. Relief overtakes Blaze, which soon turns to concern. She looks towards Judas. Only his smoking cigarette remains as Blaze feels as if someone watches her.

The sun rises as Blaze jogs along the park path. Meanwhile, Matthew, won't stop until he finds the person who killed his sister. Several young girls have gone missing, from a near-by park so Matthew starts his investigation there. He sees Blaze, who has an uncanny resemblance to his deceased sister. Matthew approaches Blaze. He warns her about the serial killer and suggests she shouldn't jog alone. Blaze pushes past Matthew. Judas looms in the morning fog.

That afternoon, Blaze meets her friends MAG and JENNI in a WI-FI café to work on a school project. When the subject of the Keystroke Killer emerges, Blaze shares her earlier encounter in the park with a stranger. This raises the curiosity between the girls just as Matthew, enters. Judas watches the interaction from afar. Blaze is uneasy about Matthew's entrance and leaves.

Later that night, Blaze prepares for bed by sipping a glass of red wine, followed by a nice hot shower to relax her. Matthew's uneasy causes him to guard Blaze's apartment from the outside. Grief overwhelms him as he looks at a picture of his sister he carries in his wallet. Judas watches them both from afar as the night turns to morning.

The next day, during Blaze's morning jog, Matthew confronts her again about the Keystroke Killer. Blaze's frustration grows with Matthew's insistence as she discards his warning. To gain her attention and trust, Matthew tells Blaze his sister was a victim of the Keystroke Killer, murdered by him less than three months ago; and she looks just like her escalating the tension between them. Judas watches from afar, as Blaze runs away from Matthew.

Judas keeps a close watch from afar on the conversation between Matthew and Blaze. Meanwhile, Mag and Jenni wait for Blaze at the WI-FI café.

Judas presses the "Delete" key on the keyboard as Mag, who leaves the WI-FI café dissolves into thin air. There is no trace of her. Judas leaves to a non-disclosed location. Shortly after, Blaze's cell phone rings.

Moments later, Matthew is more determined to rescue Blaze than before. After Blaze receives a phone call from Jenni, telling her Mag has vanished; panic overcomes her leaving Matthew to expose the truth about an unknown reality of the world created by the Keystroke Killer. Nothing will convince Blaze as she pushes past Matthew.

Later that day, Matthew breaks into Judas' home. He goes over to the computer and begins to search it.

The image of Blaze, covered in blood splatter, and a long bladed knife in her lap, pops up on the computer monitor. Matthew is horrified as if he sees a ghost from his past. He turns off the computer by pressing the "Delete" key on the keyboard. Blaze vanishes.

In anger, he pulls his gun from his holster and shoots the computer screen. Matthew heads out for revenge.

Matthew arrives at Blaze's apartment escorted by the Landlord. The apartment is blood free and there is no evidence to prove Blaze previously occupied the premises. Judas calls Matthew and informs him there is no record Blaze's existence.

Matthew, distraught from the day's events, walks along the jogging path where he first met Blaze. He carries a long-stemmed pink rose and places it on the park bench vowing to avenge her death.

That night, Matthew stands guard outside the Keystroke Killer's lair. The one man who watches others – Matthew now watches. Pulling out from his wallet his sister's picture, Matthew vows to avenge her death. He retrieves his gun. GUNSHOT. Nothing but blackness and silence remains.

To be continued ...

CHAPTER 19

THE WELL-WRITTEN SYNOPSIS

"The thing should have plot and character, beginning, middle, and end.
Arouse pity and then have a catharsis. Those were the best principles I was
ever taught." Anne Rice – New Orleans' Native Metaphysical Gothic Novelist and
Screenwriter – best known for *Interview with a Vampire*

THE PROCESS OF EDITING

We've come a long way in this book by developing a working synopsis for *The
Keystroke Killer.* However, I'm not finished. Keep in mind since the beginning of this
book I have always called it a working synopsis. It won't become finalized until I
make certain the synopsis meets all criteria and includes the key beats. I also must
edit to make certain there aren't any typographical errors, it is punctuated correctly,
and not over a page long.

The key is to edit, edit, edit, and keeping editing until it is perfect. And, did I say make sure you edit your synopsis.

USING THE BEAT SHEET

To begin the editing process, I first transfer the entire working synopsis into the Beat Sheet Evaluation Form. If you don't know what I am talking about, please refer to my book *Just Beat It!* This book explains not only how to use a beat sheet to develop a screenplay, but also how to evaluate a screenplay using a beat sheet   The form below uses the required beat descriptors I discuss in this book as it highlights the beat descriptors *The Keystroke Killer* short film below.

THE KEYSTROKE KILLER BEAT SHEET

BEATS	BEAT DESCRIPTOR
1. What would you do if the one person you loved most were erased from existence?	**Introduction of story** – Opening Image
2. Matthew, a grief stricken New York detective, lives this nightmare as he races to save BLAZE, the next victim, from the *Keystroke Killer*.	**Introduce your main character/Connector sentence**
3. Matthew grieves the only way he knows – praying for his dead sister at the park where they spent time growing up as children. It is the same park Blaze, a young college student, finds peace and solitude as she feeds ducks in the pond. As children play under their mother's careful watch, JUDAS, the Keystroke Killer, lurks in the morning mist. It's a beautiful day until TRACY, A small child, vanishes. The mother screams which catches the attention of Blaze. Moments later, the child emerges from the bathroom. Relief overtakes Blaze, which soon turns to concern. She looks towards Judas. Only his smoking cigarette remains as Blaze feels as if someone watches her. Later that day, Judas enters into his dimly lit pristine room. He watches Blaze on his computer monitor as she goes through her day. That evening, an exhausted Blaze enters her peaceful apartment occupied by her two cats. As	**Begin plot-** the set up

she pours a glass of wine, a noise startles her. She double-checks the locks on the door. There is a knock on the door and her cell phone rings. Judas watches from his computer.	
4. The sun rises as Blaze jogs along the park path. Meanwhile, MATTHEW, won't stop until he finds the person who killed his sister. Several young girls have gone missing, from a near-by park so Matthew starts his investigation there. He sees Blaze, who has an uncanny resemblance to his sister. Matthew approaches Blaze. He warns Blaze that there is a serial killer and she shouldn't jog alone. Blaze pushes pass Matthew. Judas looms in the morning fog.	**Motivation for your protagonist** – theme develops
5. That afternoon, Blaze meets her friends MAG and JENNI in a WI-FI café to work on a school project. When the subject of the Keystroke Killer emerges, Blaze shares with them her earlier encounter in the park with a stranger. This raises the curiosity between the girls just as Matthew, our stranger, enters. Judas watches the interaction from afar. Blaze is uneasy about Matthew's entrance and leaves.	**Introduce supporting character**/antagonist
6. Later that night, Blaze prepares for bed by sipping a glass of red wine, followed by a nice hot shower to relax her. Matthew's uneasiness causes him to guard Blaze's apartment from the outside. Grief overwhelms him as he looks at of his sister he carries in his wallet. Judas watches them both from afar as the night turns to morning.	**Develop the plot** – catalyst that motivates protagonist
7. The next day, during Blaze's morning jog, Matthew confronts her again about the Keystroke Killer. Blaze's frustration grows which Matthew's insistence as she discards his warning. To gain her attention and trust, Matthew tells Blaze his sister was a victim of the Keystroke Killer, murdered by him less than three months ago; and she looks just like her escalating the tension between them.	**Attraction between protagonist/antagonist**
8. Meanwhile, Mag and Jenni wait for Blaze at the WI-FI café. As Judas watches Mag and Jennie, he also keeps a close watch on Matthew and Blaze.	**The plot thickens** – protagonist doubtful of outcome
9. Judas presses the "Delete" key on the keyboard and Mag, who leaves the WI-FI café, dissolves into thin air. There is no trace of her. Judas leaves to a non-disclosed location. Shortly	**Up the Stakes** – antagonist throws things at protagonist

after, Blaze's cell phone rings.	
10. Moments later, Matthew is more determined to rescue Blaze than before. After Blaze receives a phone call from Jennie telling her Mag has vanished, panic overcomes her leaving Matthew to expose the truth about an unknown reality of the world created by the Keystroke Killer. Nothing convinces Blaze as she pushes past Matthew.	**Reaction of your antagonist** – more things thrown
11. Later that day, Matthew breaks into the lair of the Keystroke Killer. He goes over to the computer and begins to search it.	**Resolution by protagonist** – overcomes problem
12. The image of Blaze covered in blood splatter with a long bladed knife in her lap pops up on the screen. Matthew is horrified as if he sees a ghost from his past. He turns off the computer by pressing the "Delete" key on the keyboard. Blaze vanishes.	**Dark moment/no way out** – antagonist and protagonist battle
13. In anger, Matthew pulls his gun from his holster and shoots the computer screen. Matthew heads out for revenge.	**Build anticipation** – audience uncertain of outcome
14. Matthew arrives to Blaze's apartment escorted by the Landlord. The apartment is blood free and there is no evidence to prove Blaze previously occupied the premises. Judas calls Matthew and informs him there is no record of Blaze's existence. The landlord confirms that no one has occupied the apartment for more than a year.	**Regaining control** – protagonist regains control – learns something new
15. Matthew, distraught from the day's events, walks along the jogging path where he first met Blaze. He carries a long-stemmed pink rose and places it on the park bench vowing to avenge her death.	**Final resolution** – problem solved/or counter resolution (cliff-hanger)
16. That night, Matthew stands guard outside the Keystroke Killer's lair. The one man who watches others – Matthew now watches. Pulling out from his wallet his sister's picture, Matthew vows to avenge her death. He retrieves his gun. GUNSHOT. Nothing but blackness and silence remain.	**Ending** – how the protagonist changed from the beginning

MARTINI SYNOPSIS

Making sure your synopsis is perfect is much like the martini shot for a film shoot. Before the director can call for the martini shot, or last shot, he has to make sure that all coverage is clear. That means every scene and all dialogue captured onto film prior to "moving on" or closing the set permanently. It's a lengthy process and requires numerous crewmembers checking in with the director, which usually is handed off to the first assistant director. The developing synopsis up to this point is the "Martini Synopsis." I can't call for "Check the gate," until all aspects for a well-constructed synopsis is in place.

Just Beat it!

Make certain to include all beat points in the plot by placing the working synopsis onto a beat sheet. If you need help or clarification on beat sheets, remember I have the book *Just Beat it* in my quick guidebook series on this topic. If any component is missing, I first check to make sure the beat occurs in the screenplay. If I didn't, I will rewrite the section of the screenplay to include it and then modify the synopsis accordingly.

Use the "Martini Shot" process when writing every synopsis. Just as crewmembers from the camera, hair, assistant director, script supervisor departments, the beat sheet becomes your check and balance for your final synopsis. That way, making certain all elements are included in screenplay and the synopsis too. One benefit of this approach is you get a chronological order of your action in your screenplay. It makes my job easier when I sit down to write a synopsis.

The Blueprint

In this entire book, I demonstrate how I develop the synopsis for *The Keystroke Killer*. Now, I put it all together. When writing my synopsis, I write individual paragraphs, and then join them where it is appropriate. I try to write the final synopsis in a five-paragraph blueprint structure from the beat sheet:

- Paragraph 1 - Opening
- Paragraph 2 - Act I
- Paragraph 3 - Act II
- Paragraph 4 - Act III
- Paragraph 5 - Resolution and the final image.

One is Enough

A synopsis fits on a single page and covers the screenplay from the beginning to the end. If your synopsis goes over a page, then it has developed into a treatment. Both a synopsis and treatment are narratives. However, you must remove any extraneous information, sub-plots, and minor characters from a synopsis. A treatment will often include these. Therefore, the next stage is to narrow the synopsis to fit on a single page. Keep in mind that this book's format is an 8 X 10 inch page and not the standard 8.5 X 11 inch that you present a synopsis to others. For inclusion in the book, the sections regarding the synopsis development are indented. Additionally, because of the print, the spacing between the sentences is 1.5 lines instead of single-spaced to make the book easier to read. Therefore, the format of my book makes the synopsis look as if it is more than one page. When I transfer my synopsis onto standard size paper, with .5-inch margins, and single space between the sentences, it fits onto a single letter size piece of paper (pictured to the left). Please keep that in mind when you read my final synopsis.

Unfortunately, narrowing a synopsis to a single page is difficult. You have to make the decision of what to cut to make it fit. Cutting too much can have a detrimental effect on the overall presentation and content. When deciding on words to cut, DO NOT cut your final image. If anything, cut something out of Act II and any extraneous information in the action description, subplots, and supporting characters. Research has proven most people will read the first paragraph, skim the middle, and read the end. This tip should provide you with a guideline when narrowing your synopsis.

Dot the "I" and Cross the "T"

Spell and grammar checking your synopsis is critical. However, don't rely on a software program as your main editing option. It could lead you astray. Many times, you might use a word such as "There" when you meant to write the word "Their." If you spell check your document, the software program won't pick up this error because the initial word was spelt correctly. The same holds true for words spelled alike, but only one letter is changed. For example, the words "Word" and "Work." Making a typographical error like this occurs all of the time and difficult to determine.

I find it is easier to proof another person's work rather than my own. Just ask my copy proof editor Robby Stroud. She laughs at me all the time when I accidently type "the" when it should have been "they" or misspelled "guarantee" by reversing the "a" and the "u." Trust me when I say, it is very easy to make a mistake and then proof your own writing. I think other authors would agree with me. Therefore, take it from an experienced author and rely on someone else to help you edit your synopsis. Make sure to dot all "I's" and cross all "T's." Make every word count and pay attention to detail. This means to check all of your work to make sure it is correct which includes even the seemingly insignificant things you might otherwise overlook. I'll provide the following as an example. When writing *The Keystroke Killer*, I initially used Final Draft. When I typed the following slug line, "INT. KEYSTROKE LAIR – NIGHT," it seemed harmless enough. It wasn't until the second book in this series that I caught the typing error. Instead of "KEYSTROKE," I typed "KEYSTOKE."

It's amazing how many times I read *The Keystroke Killer* in writing the guidebook series. Again, it wasn't until this book that I caught the error. Fortunately, I decided to publish all three books at the same time so I was able to make the change before publication in each book. That's how the simplest "insignificant" things can be overlooked. You get accustomed to looking at a word and all of a sudden, it begins to look right to you. Moreover, the most frustrating thing of all was that spell check didn't catch it.

HOW TO PRESENT YOUR SYNOPSIS

Industry standards dictate the presentation and style of your synopsis. To make certain you get you screenplay into the hands of agents, managers, and producers, use the following format guidelines when presenting your synopsis.

Format
- Limit to a single page.
- Use one-inch margins.
- Use no less than 12-point font of either Courier or Times Roman.
- Single-space the paragraphs.
- Double space between each paragraph and the title.
- In the header section of the page type your name and contact information. Be sure to include a phone number and your email address.
- In the footer section, include the words "Synopsis of (TITLE OF SCRIPT). Beneath that put the WGA number and/or copyright information.
- Generate a cover page with your contact information and a place for you to write a personal note to the reader.
- If space allows, include your logline prior to the presentation of your synopsis.

FINAL TIPS

Here are some key points to consider when you get ready to write your final synopsis.

- Make sure all beat points are in the synopsis
- Every sentence is a complete sentence
- No typographical errors
- Remove extraneous information

The next two pages is an example of the cover page and the final synopsis for *The Keystroke Killer*.

Sample Cover Sheet 1

SYNOPSIS

LOGLINE: After Matthew realizes Blaze is the next target of a serial killer, his attempt to expose him proves fatal.

Screenwriter: Dr. Melissa Caudle
Copyright © 2011
drmelcaudle@gmail.com **555-255-3245**
12-3-2011

FOR MORE INFORMATION CONTACT
ON THE LOT PRODUCTIONS
WWW.ONTHELOTPRODUCTIONS.COM
555-588-4589

Email: Project@onthelot@gmail.com

THE KEYSTROKE KILLER

What would you do if the one person you loved most were erased from existence? MATTHEW, a grief stricken New York detective, lives this nightmare as he races to save BLAZE, the next victim, from the KEYSTROKE KILLER. Matthew grieves the only way he knows – praying for his dead sister at the park where they spent time growing up as children. It is the same park Blaze, a young college student, finds peace and solitude as she feeds ducks in the pond. As children play under their mother's careful watch, JUDAS, aka the Keystroke Killer, lurks in the morning mist. A MOTHER screams catching Blaze's attention. The child emerges from the bathroom. Blaze looks towards Judas but only his smoking cigarette remains.

The next day, Matthew sees Blaze, who has an uncanny resemblance to his deceased sister, jogging in the park. Matthew warns her about the serial killer and suggests she should not jog alone. Blaze pushes past Matthew as Judas looms in the morning fog. That afternoon, Blaze meets her friends MAG and JENNI in a WI-FI café to work on a school project. When the subject of the Keystroke Killer emerges, Blaze shares her earlier encounter with Matthew. This raises the curiosity between the girls just as he enters. Judas watches the interaction from afar. Blaze is uneasy about Matthew's entrance and leaves. Later that night, Blaze prepares for bed by sipping a glass of red wine, followed by a nice hot shower to relax her. Matthew's uneasy causes him to guard Blaze's apartment from the outside. Grief overwhelms him as he looks at a picture of his sister he carries in his wallet. Judas watches them both from his lair as the night turns to morning.

The sun rises as Blaze's jogs along the path. Matthew confronts her again as her frustration grows. She discards his warning. To gain her attention and trust, Matthew reveals his sisters murder by the Keystroke Killer less than three months ago. Judas watches from his lair the conversation between Matthew and Blaze. Meanwhile, Mag and Jenni wait for Blaze at the WI-FI café. Judas presses the "Delete" key on the keyboard as Mag, who leaves the WI-FI café dissolves into thin air. There is no trace of her. Judas leaves to a non-disclosed location. Moments later, Matthew is more determined to rescue Blaze than before. After Blaze receives a phone call from Jenni, panic overcomes her leaving Matthew to expose the truth about the Keystroke Killer. Nothing convinces Blaze as she pushes past Matthew.

Later that day, Matthew breaks into the Keystroke Killer's lair. He goes over to the computer and begins to search it. The image of Blaze, covered in blood splatter, and a long bladed knife in her lap, pops up on the computer monitor. Matthew is horrified as if he sees a ghost from his past. He turns off the computer by pressing the "Delete" key on the keyboard. Blaze vanishes. In anger, he pulls his gun from his holster and shoots the computer screen. Matthew heads out for revenge to Blaze's apartment. Upon arrival, the apartment is blood free and no evidence trace to prove Blaze previously occupied the premises. Judas calls Matthew and informs him there is no record Blaze's existence.

Matthew, distraught from the day's events, walks along the jogging path where he first saw Blaze. He carries a long-stemmed pink rose and places it on the park bench vowing to avenge her death. That night, Matthew stands guard outside the lair. The one man who watches others – Matthew now watches. He retrieves from his wallet his sister's picture and vows to avenge her death. He un-holsters his gun. GUNSHOT. Nothing but blackness and silence remains. Matthew lives with the truth.

HOW TO VARY YOUR SYNOPSIS

One of the great things about brainstorming options for each section of the synopsis is the variety. You have the option to create multiply synopses by replacing different sentences created during the developmental stage. Thereby, you can create different versions.

When you send out your synopsis, keep a record on a "Dissemination List" of which one you sent to determine if one gets more responses than the rest. That way you know which synopsis obtains the best result. Format your dissemination list by using the suggested columns below.

SYNOPSIS VERSION	DATE SENT	WHO IT WAS SENT TO	RESULT/FEEDBACK
Version 1	12-4-2011	Screen Gems – Blake Dominion, 1112 Wilshire Blvd. Los Angeles, CA 90012	Send screenplay
Version 2	12-8-2011	On the Edge Studio, 45 5th Street, New York, NY	Haven't heard back
Version 2	1-16-2012	Bootstrap Productions, 3345 Milhouse Road, NY, NY	Asked for business plan
Version 1	1-25-2012	Purple Dot Entertainment, 890 Filmore Lane, Ste. 12, San Francisco, CA	Send one pager and screenplay.
Version 3	1-30-2012	Universal Studios, 1212 Wilshire Blvd., Los Angeles, CA 90012	Haven't heard back

Look at the version 2 of the synopsis created for *The Keystroke Killer* using the different brainstorming sentences at each development stage and editing to make the sentences flow. I also have added the logline to the cover sheet.

Cover Sample 2

SYNOPSIS

Haunted by his sister's death, a New York Detective takes revenge against the killer.

Written by Dr. Melissa Caudle
Copyright © 2011
drmelcaudle@gmail.com **555-255-3245**
12-3-2011

WWW.ONTHELOTPRODUCTIONS.COM   **Email:** Project@onthelot@gmail.com

THE KEYSTROKE KILLER
Written by Dr. Melissa Caudle

What would you do if you discovered the human race wasn't real? After his sister's death, MATTHEW, a grieving New York detective, discovers the truth behind her killer. It all began one morning in a local park. He sees Blaze, who has an uncanny resemblance to his sister. His intuition tells him Blaze is the next target of the Keystroke Killer and develops a plan to save her.

Later that day, two of Blaze's closest friends, MAG and JENNI join her at their favorite study place – The WI-FI Café. They talk about a serial killer who stalks girls in a nearby park. Anxiety emerges when Blaze tells the girls that a strange man approached her in the park that morning. Moments later, Matthew enters and Blaze rushes out. Meanwhile, Judas watches the interaction on his computer monitor from his lair. That night, Blaze is safe in her apartment after having a difficult day. She follows her nightly routine by pouring a glass of red wine followed by a hot shower. Matthew stands below her window staring and waiting to protect her. He pulls a picture from his wallet of his sister. As night turns to morning, Judas watches them both from his lair.

The sun rises over the park as Blaze endures her morning jog. Matthew stands nearby and waits for the perfect moment to confront her. Blaze jogs closer and Matthew stands. His movement startles her. He reveals to her that she is going to be the next victim of the Keystroke Killer. She discards Matthew's information with indignation. She thinks he is a freak and runs as fast as she can away from him. He yells back to her that she looks just like his dead sister who was murdered. Matthew continues to try to convince her that she is going to be the next victim. Meanwhile, Jenni and Mag wait for Blaze at The WI-FI café. Judas watches from his lair. Out of frustration, Mag leaves. She's tired of waiting on Blaze. Under the careful watch of Judas, Blaze and Matthew continue their conversation in the park. Judas, while sitting at his computer presses the "Delete" key on the keyboard. Mag vanishes. Blackness and static noise prevail. Back at the park, Blaze receives a phone call from Jenni informing her that Mag has disappeared. Matthew continues to try to convince Blaze. When he tells her the world isn't real, she panics. Determined to save her from the Keystroke Killer, Matthew is more persistent. He tells Blaze he can show her the truth. Blaze runs.

Distraught by Blaze's rejection, Matthew has one choice – to investigate Judas. He breaks into the lair and discovers shocking contents on Judas' computer monitor. Blaze is dead and covered with blood splatter. Her knife lay across her lap. The once determined Matthew shows fear. He has failed. He reflects on his sister's picture and then rushes from Judas lair. Blaze's apartment is empty. No trace of Blaze remains. Matthew, escorted by the LANDLORD enters the apartment. The Landlord informs Matthew that no one has lived in the apartment for over a year just as he receives a phone call from Judas. Judas reveals that there is no evidence to support the existence of Blaze. Grief overpowers Matthew as he reflects on the deaths of Blaze and his sister. He returns to the park and places a long-stemmed pink rose on the park bench where he first saw Blaze. He vows to take down the Keystroke Killer.

Under dimly lit streetlights, Matthew stands guard below the lair. Revenge is prominent across his face. He pulls the picture of his sister from his wallet. When Judas crosses in front of the window, Matthew pulls a gun. GUN SHOT. The gunfire reverbs. Blackness surrounds the mist floating up toward the lights, which fades to darkness and silence.

A PENNY FOR YOUR THOUGHTS

After reading the second version of the synopsis for *The Keystroke Killer*, what do you think? Which version do you like? Is version one stronger than version two? The reason for asking is to get you to think about developing your own synopsis for a screenplay. Formulate various versions. Keep writing and revising until you get one or two that you absolutely love. Have several of your respected friends and family members read them ask them which one they like. Send me your two versions. I'll read them and if I have time, I'll respond back and tell you which one I like.

PROTECTING YOUR WORK

Stay honest and protect yourself. It is important to remember that you can't copyright an idea; you can only copyright a written document. There are plenty of screenplays available about a serial killer. I can't copyright that idea. However, my screenplay *The Keystroke Killer* I can.

Most new screenwriters are scared their work is going to be stolen. Yes, it can happen. However, I seriously doubt it will. Agents, managers, and producers aren't in the business of stealing screenplays. Frankly, there are 100,000 screenplays to choose in today's market. They don't need to steal one to film one. So don't be afraid to let people read your screenplay once you have registered it with The Writer's Guild of America (WGA). The cost is $20. To me, that is inexpensive for my own piece of mind.

To save money, you can copyright your logline, synopsis, treatment, and screenplay in the same document. However, I always register my screenplay separately.

DO'S AND DON'TS OF A WELL-WRITTEN SYNOPSIS

DO
- Start with a hook
- Introduce your characters
- Provide motivation
- Construct the body of your synopsis with the key elements

- Limit your synopsis to three to four paragraphs and one page (anything more than that it becomes a treatment.)
- Always write in present tense
- Always answer the who, what, when, where and why
- Use strong action verbs and high-stake adjectives
- Throw in sample statements made by the character
- Make every word count
- Take out the fluff
- Re-write, re-write, and then re-write it again.
- Proofread your synopsis

DON'T

- State your opinion
- Use words no one understands
- Be to wordy
- Over simplify your plot
- Go over one page
- Write in a passive voice or past tense
- Use clichés
- State where it is located unless it is prevalent to the plot
- Write about every character unless they are critical to the turning points of your screenplay
- Use detailed prose as you would in a novel.

YOUR TURN

Please give me your feedback and tell me what you think of the synopsis included in this book for *The Keystroke Killer*; or write one of your own and send it to me at drmelcaudle@gmail.com.

www.onthelotproductions.com

Additionally, any filmmaker may use the screenplay *The Keystroke Killer* to produce a short film as long as you do three things:

1. Give me credit as the screenwriter in the opening title credits, your website, poster, DVD, and on IMDB.

2. Invite me to set when you are filming at drmelcaudle@gmail.com. Who knows, you might get me as a free production assistant for the day. No promises, but if I'm available, it has happened before.
3. Send me a DVD of the completed film.

THE KSK TELEVISION SERIES

I am interested in reading what you as a screenwriter can do in terms of writing a spec sequel script for *The Keystroke Killer*. Remember that I am turning this into a television series; therefore, need 62 episodes to complete a five-year deal, no longer than 45 pages each. *The Keystroke Killer* and the characters created are copyright protected and trademarked. However, I encourage your spec script submissions based off my screenplay. The parameters for the spec script are:

• No longer than 45 pages

• You must register your script with the WGA or U.S. Library of Congress. Neither my production company, my publisher, nor I can accept responsibility for unregistered scripts and we not read them.

• Include a cover sheet with the title, episode name, screenwriter's name, contact information, and WGA registration number.

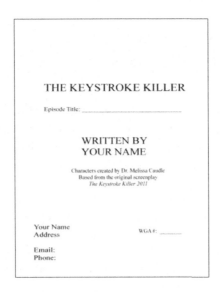

Sample Cover Sheet for KSK Submission

- Correctly formatted; e.g., scene number, slug line, action description, dialogue (Final Draft or Celtx is the best to use)

Sample Scene Format

44. EXT. THE KEYSTROKE KILLER LAIR – NIGHT

Matthew walks up to the outside of the Keystroke Killer's lair and stands guard. If looks could kill, Judas would be dead.

Matthew pulls out his wallet and looks at the picture of his sister as Judas passes in front of the window.

                         MATTHEW
                  This is far from over.

GUN SHOT.

- Each spec script should have its own title to reflect your episode. Every title should begin with "KSK" followed by something catchy that encompasses the plot of the episode.

  Format
  KSK: _____.

  Example Titles
  KSK: Pandora's Box
  KSK: Bad Luck Blues
  KSK: Beneath Still Waters

- Must include Matthew searching for the Keystroke Killer's identity. Although he discovered the lair, Judas has now vacated it and moved to another secret location. Matthew continues to search for him throughout the series to avenge his sister's death as well as Blaze's.

- You can use flashbacks from the original screenplay.

- You can write a brand new scene showing the murder of Matthew's sister, them as children in the park, or talking etc. Since she resides in the fourth dimension, she could "punch" her way to our dimension and try to make contact through an electronic device.

- Blaze can also try to "punch" through to our dimension and cry for help.

- CANNOT reveal the Keystroke Killer's face or identity.

- Remember that the Keystroke Killer resides in a fourth dimension and he can only interact with our world by taking the possession of a human being. You can include scenes in the fourth dimension or the possession of another body.

- You can have Blaze haunt Matthew (She becomes his conscience as his check and balance when she finally punches through to our dimension). This gives him hope to keep searching for his sister.

- Mag does or does not have to be included.

- New Characters, returning or one-time appearance may be created.

- Matthew can develop a love interest.

- Matthew can have a partner.

- Each spec script must have another person vanishing as a result of the Keystroke Killer. This is what keeps Matthew in the game.

If a network, as a part of this series, produces your spec script, you will receive payment according to their payment schedule. You will not be paid to submit a spec script and this should in no way be misconstrued as an offering to appropriate your screenplay. This is **not** an offer of employment, nor can I guarantee the production of your script. Moreover, On the Lot Productions, LLC, nor can I as the author of this book will be responsible for any liabilities involving coincidental

similarities to works-in-progress or other submissions. The script is currently being shopped to Fox and Sci Fy. To find out how to submit your spec script, refer to the Appendix section that provides the instructions on how to submit a script. Please register your spec scripts with the WGA.

MY TURN

Your synopsis could be used featured on my production website located at www.onthelotproductions.com if you choose to write one for *The Keystroke Killer*. If you do decide to produce *The Keystroke Killer,* I will gladly give you free advice, and we can use Skype to communicate.

If you'd like, I already have the script broken down with a shooting schedule. If you want to use that to save time, just email me at drmelcaudle@gmail.com and request it. It's free. That's just an option for you, but not mandatory. This is a great way for you to show me what your production team can do.

Once you complete filming of your version of the short film *The Keystroke Killer*, I will announce it in my newsletter and send out an email blast to those on my social network sites and to my family and friends so they can watch it and you will get new viewers. I will also use my Facebook page and my Twitter account to tweet about it. To join my newsletter visit www.therealityofrealitytv.com.

If your production of *The Keystroke Killer* it is outstanding, I'll encourage you to submit it to film festivals and possibly consider your team for a future production for an On the Lot Productions, LLC feature film, and link your version to my production website.

Take a chance and produce *The Keystroke Killer*. It can be a lot of fun for all of us.

THE KEYSTROKE KILLER FACEBOOK SITE

I have created a Facebook page for fans of *The Keystroke Killer*. Go there and discuss it with fellow supporters.

@

THE KEYSTROKE KILLER FAN SITE

THE KEYSTROKE KILLER MERCHANDISE CENTER

If you are really a fan of *The Keystroke Killer*, I have lots of merchandise available from *The Keystroke Killer* and my other films that include:

- T-Shirts
- Coffee Mugs
- Mouse Pad
- Keychain
- Poster

Purchase your items today from www.onthelotproductions.com.

PHOTOGRAPHY CREDITS

Numerous people have contributed photographs for the illustrations provided in this book. I cannot thank them enough for their contributions and I want to credit each of them. Likewise, www.freedigitalphotos.net provided photographs used with permission from the website.   I have taken every effort to ensure that each photographer or creator receives credit for his or her graphic design or photograph. I apologize in advance if I have made any errors. This was not my intent.

FRONT COVER DESIGN
Front Jacket Cover designed by Open Door Publishing House in conjunction with Dr. Mel Caudle

FRONT COVER FILMSTRIP TOP MONTAGE FROM LEFT TO RIGHT PHOTO CREDIT
Lovers by Kong Sky
A.D.A.M. Graphic by On the Lot Productions, LLC
Greece photo by Erin Gamvrogianis
Pulse Graphic by On the Lot Productions, LLC
Ferris Wheel by BJ Wok
Hollywood Sign by Porbital
Never Stop Running Graphic by On the Lot Productions, LLC - Ticking Time Piece by Michael Warner
Jamie Alyson by Dr. Mel Caudle
Taxi Cab by Mantas Ruzveltas

FRONT COVER FILMSTRIP BOTTOM MONTAGE FROM LEFT TO RIGHT PHOTO CREDIT
African Women by Africa @freedigitalphotos.net
Secret Romances Graphic by On the Lot Productions, LLC
Pendulum by Michael Warner
Exile Graphic by On the Lot Productions, LLC
Motorcycle Cross Rider by Toa55 @freedigitalphotos.net
Stealth Launch Site by Dr. Mel Caudle
The Other Man Graphic by On the Lot Productions, LLC
Plane by Tim Beach
Downtown Graphic by On the Lot Productions, LLC
Woman on Rock by Michael Warner

BOOK COVERS FOR GUIDEBOOK SERIES PHOTO CREDIT
How to Write a Logline, Synopsis, and One Pager for Films and Reality TV designed by Open Door Publishing House in conjunction with Dr. Mel Caudle
How to Write a Logline: Quick Guidebook for Screenwriters designed by Open Door Publishing House in conjunction with Dr. Mel Caudle
How to Create a One Pager: Quick Guidebook for Screenwriters designed by Open Door Publishing House in conjunction with Dr. Mel Caudle
How to Write a Synopsis: Quick Guidebook for Screenwriters designed by Open Door Publishing House in conjunction with Dr. Mel Caudle

ACKNOWLEDGEMENT PHOTO CREDIT
Dr. Mel Caudle photo by Tim Moree

SPECIAL THANKS PHOTO CREDIT
Jamie Alyson and Dr. Mel in Limo by Robby Stroud

INTRODUCTION - WHAT'S UP WITH THAT PHOTO CREDIT
Logos for all five films created by On the Lot Productions, LLC
Brain Freeze created by On the Lot Productions, LLC
Pencil Erasing "Edit Wrong Word" by Ning Milo
Earth and Mouse with The Keystroke Killer created by On the Lot Productions, LLC, Earth and Mouse photo by XEDOS4 @freedigitalphotos.net
How to Write a Logline, Synopsis, and One Pager for Films and Reality TV designed by Open Door Publishing House in conjunction with Dr. Mel Caudle
How to Write a Logline: Quick Guidebook for Screenwriters designed by Open Door Publishing House in conjunction with Dr. Mel Caudle
How to Create a One Pager: Quick Guidebook for Screenwriters designed by Open Door Publishing House in conjunction with Dr. Mel Caudle
The Keystroke Killer Screenplay Cover created by On the Lot Productions, LLC – Photo of Jamie Alyson by Hoda Hahn, Knife with Blood by Simon Howden
The Keystroke Killer Inside the Writer's Mind Cover created by On the Lot Productions, LLC – Photo of Jamie Alyson by Hoda Hahn, Knife with Blood by Simon Howden

CHAPTER 1 – THE POWER OF A SYNOPSIS PHOTO CREDIT
Man with Light Bulb Head by Chan Pipat
Clock on Money by Renjith Krishran
Money on a Hook by Scott Chan
Bent Nails by Boaz Yiftach
Smoking by Graur Codrin
The Keystroke Killer Graphic created by On the Lot Productions, LLC – Photo of Knife with Blood by Simon Howden, Earth by Idea Go
On the Lot Productions, LLC Logo by Melanie Bledsoe

CHAPTER 2 – THE KEYSTROKE KILLER PHOTO CREDIT
The Keystroke Killer Post Card One Pager created by On the Lot Productions, LLC – Blood by Simon
PG -13 created by On the Lot Productions, LLC
Follow Us on Facebook used with permission of Facebook.com
The Keystroke Killer Screenplay Cover created by On the Lot Productions, LLC – Photo of Jamie Alyson by Hoda Hahn, Knife with Blood by Simon Howden

CHAPTER 3 – THE SYNOPSIS CONVERSATION PHOTO CREDIT
Jamie Alyson by Dr. Mel Caudle
Jamie Alyson by Hoda Hahn
Dr. Mel on Skype taken by Dr. Mel from her webcam

CHAPTER 4 – THE OPENER PHOTO CREDIT
Dice Question by JZ Creationz
Clock by Matthew Morris
Matthew by Salvatore Vuono
World Map by Digital Art
Matthew by Salvatore Vuono
Reflection on the Tomb created by On the Lot Productions, LLC – Jamie Alyson photo by Dr. Mel Caudle, Grave photo by Topset07@freedigitalphotos.net
The Keystroke Killer Graphic created by On the Lot Productions, LLC – Photo Earth by Idea Go
Bridge by Exsodus@freedigitalphotos.net
Grieving Matthew by Salvatore Vuono

CHAPTER 5 – THE SET UP PHOTO CREDIT
Hay by Roland Darby
Criminal Minds Screenplay Autographed by Dr. Mel Caudle
Needle in a Haystack by Gary Brown
Rolling Credits by On the Lot Productions, LLC – featuring Jamie Alyson as Blaze
Mother and Child on Playground by Photo Stock used with permission
Pine Cone and Needles by Maggie Smith

CHAPTER 6 - MOTIVATION STATEMENT PHOTO CREDIT
Smoking Matthew by Salvatore Vuono
In His Head created by On the Lot Productions, LLC – photo of Matthew by Salvatore Vuono, Jamie Alyson by Dr. Mel Caudle, and Cross at Grave by Topset07 @freedigitalphotos.net
Matthew's Desk in the Bullpen provided by On the Lot Productions, LLC
Detective Badge photo still provided by On the Lot Productions, LLC
Misty Morning by Dan @freedigitalphotos.net

CHAPTER 7 - THE ANTAGONIST
Villain from Never Stop Running provided by On the Lot Productions, LLC
Blaze at the Computer provided by On the Lot Productions, LLC

CHAPTER 8 – CONTINUING PLOT PHOTO CREDIT
Blaze provided by On the Lot Productions, LLC

CHAPTER 9 – THE GREAT ATTRACTION PHOTO CREDIT
The Keystroke Killer Screenplay Cover created by On the Lot Productions, LLC – Photo of Jamie Alyson by Hoda Hahn, Matthew by Salvatore Vuono, Earth and Eye by Idea Go
Magnet by Danilo Rizzuti
Treatise on Electricity and Magnetism book cover provided publicdomain.com
Jogger provided by On the Lot Productions, LLC

CHAPTER 10 – THE PLOT THICKENS PHOTO CREDIT
Graphic created by On the Lot Productions, LLC – photo of Matthew by Salvatore Vuono, Jamie Alyson by Hoda Hahn, and Magic Ball by Raymond Rizzoto
Judas at Computer by Photo Stock used with permission

CHAPTER 11 – UP THE STAKES PHOTO CREDIT
The Keystroke Killer Screenplay Cover created by On the Lot Productions, LLC – Photo of Jamie Alyson by Hoda Hahn, Matthew by Salvatore Vuono, Earth and Eye by Eedos4@freedigitalphotos.net

CHAPTER 12 – REACTION PHOTO CREDIT
Matthew by Salvatore Vuono

CHAPTER 13 – BRINGING RESOLUTION
Graphic created by On the Lot Productions – photo of Jamie Alyson by Hoda Hahn, Eye Over Earth by Idea Go, Matthew by Salvatore Vuono, New York by Putt Sky and Jamie Alyson by Hoda Hahn

CHAPTER 14– DARK MOMENT PHOTO CREDIT
Bloody Knife by Simon Howden
The Keystroke Killer Graphic created by On the Lot Productions, LLC – Photo of Knife with Blood by Simon Howden, Jamie Alyson by Hoda Hahn

CHAPTER 15 – FILLED WITH ANTICIPATION PHOTO CREDIT
Anticipation of Christmas Morning by Dr. Mel Caudle
Christmas Ornaments by Dr. Mel Caudle
Fries and Ketchup by Keerati@freedigitalphotos.net
Simon and Garfunkel Album Cover provided by The Apple Music Store Collection of Collectable Albums
Snail by Simon Howden
Gun Shot by Steve Horder

CHAPTER 16 – REGAIN CONTROL PHOTO CREDIT
Graphic created by On the Lot Productions, LLC – photo remote control by Steven Valenci, Earth photo and bloody knife photo by Simon Howden

CHAPTER 17 – THE FINAL COUNTDOWN PHOTO CREDIT
Graphic created by On the Lot Productions, LLC – photo of space shuttle provided by NASA
New Orleans Saints Super Bowl Ring photo footage by On the Lot Productions, LLC
Dolphins player during Super Bowl VII photo by Nathan B. Stark from his archive collection attending Super Bowls
Tackle on Matthew Shaub photo by Scott Peterson III – super fan of the Texans
Outage at NFL Game of Vikings and Giants photo by Mary Callahan – super fan of the Vikings
Park Bench by Simon Howden
Bloody Rose by Simon Howden

CHAPTER 18 – HAPPILY EVER AFTER
Graphic created by On the Lot Productions, LLC – photo of lovers by Kong Sky

CHAPTER 19 – THE WELL-WRITTEN SYNOPSIS PHOTO CREDIT
The Keystroke Killer One Pager Post Card created by On the Lot Productions, LLC – photos from left to right are: Jamie Alyson by Hoda Hahn, New York by Putt Sky, Matthew by Salvatore Vuono, Jamie Alyson by Hoda Hahn
The Keystroke Killer Graphic created by On the Lot Productions, LLC – Photo Earth by Idea Go, bloody knife by Simon Howden

ABOUT THE AUTHOR PHOTO CREDIT
Dr. Mel Caudle Portrait by Matthew Douglas

FOLLOW DR. MEL PHOTO CREDIT
Dr. Mel Caudle Portrait by Matthew Douglas

APPENDIX PHOTO CREDIT
How to Write a Logline, Synopsis, and One Pager for Films and Reality TV designed by Open Door Publishing House in conjunction with Dr. Mel Caudle
How to Write a Logline: Quick Guidebook for Screenwriters designed by Open Door Publishing House in conjunction with Dr. Mel Caudle
How to Create a One Pager: Quick Guidebook for Screenwriters designed by Open Door Publishing House in conjunction with Dr. Mel Caudle
How to Write a Synopsis: A Quick Guidebook for Screenwriters designed by Open Door Publishing House in conjunction with Dr. Mel Caudle
Writing Press Releases: Get Your Reality Show in the News designed by Open Door Publishing House in conjunction with Dr. Mel Caudle
Fundraising for Low-Budget Films designed by Open Door Publishing House in conjunction with Dr. Mel Caudle
The Film Production Coordinator designed by Open Door Publishing House in conjunction with Dr. Mel Caudle
How to Format a Reality Show designed by Open Door Publishing House in conjunction with Dr. Mel Caudle
The Art of the Production Coordinator: Impress for Success! designed by Open Door Publishing House in conjunction with Dr. Mel Caudle
The Reality of Reality TV: Reality Show Business Plans created by On the Lot Productions, LLC

The Reality of Reality TV: Workbook created by On the Lot Productions, LLC
The Reality of Reality TV: Reality Show Business Plans Template created by On the Lot Productions, LLC
150 Ways to Fund a Reality Show created by On the Lot Productions, LLC
Reality Show Handbook created by On the Lot Productions, LLC
The Reality Show Resource Logo created by On the Lot Productions, LLC
A New Era of Screenwriting Ad created by Open Door Publishing House
Dr. Mel Caudle portrait by Tim Moree

INDEX

ABOUT THE AUTHOR

Dr. Melissa Caudle earned a PhD in statistical research and administration from the University of New Orleans. She is a retired award winning high school principal who came into the television and film production arena in 1986 when she was on the morning news with a live episode talk-format segment dealing with educational issues for children. Capitalizing on her educational training and background, she uses her experience and training to bring her readers information that is easy to understand; yet, comprehensive. Her books for screenwriters, producers, and reality show creators are fast becoming the number resources around the globe. Never before, has there been a more accomplished individual to share information. From her book *The Reality of Reality TV: Film Business Plans,* to her "how to books," Dr. Mel provides instruction and insight for her readers. She also published numerous books for screenwriters and reality show creators including *150 Ways to Fund a Reality Show, The Reality Show Handbook, Funding for Low-Budget Films,* and *How to Get Your Reality Show in the News.* Additional books are forthcoming in the winter of 2012 including the much-anticipated books *The Art of the Production Coordinator* and *The Film Production Travel Coordinator.*

Dr. Mel is also a feature and documentary filmmaker; including *Mexico Missions, The Dolphins in Terry Cove, The Alabama Gulf Coast Zoo, Sean Kelly's Irish Pub, Beauvoir,* and *Voices of the Innocent.* Her film credits include producer on the independent film *Dark Blue* and associate producer on the films *Varla Jean and the Mushroomheads* and *Girls Gone Gangsta.* Dr. Mel has worked on films such as the two Sony films, *STRAWDOGS* starring Kate Bosworth, James Marsden, and Alexander Skarsgard; *MARDI GRAS* starring Carmen Electra and Josh Gad; *On the Seventh Day* with Blair Underwood, Pam Grier, Sharon Leal, and Jamie Alyson; and *Dirty Politics* starring Melissa Peterman, Beau Bridges, and Judd Nelson. She also has been a program director for a television station in Alabama. Her company, On the Lot Productions, LLC is currently in pre-production on several feature films and reality show projects. She has written ten screenplays and created five reality shows. Dr. Mel currently lives in New Orleans, LA, is married to Mike Caudle. She has three daughters, three sons-in-laws, and is the proud grandmother of three grandsons.

FOLLOW DR. MELISSA CAUDLE

Email: drmelcaudle@gmail.com

SOCIAL NETWORKING
Twitter: Melissa Caudle
Facebook: Melissa Ray Caudle
Facebook: The Reality of Reality TV
Facebook: The Keystroke Killer Fan Site

OFFICIAL WEBSITES
www.onthelotproductions.com
www.therealityofrealitytv.com
www.therealitytvresource.com
www.drmelcaudle.com

**JOIN UP FOR DR. MEL'S FREE NEWSLETTER
WWW.THEREALITYOFREALITYTV.COM**

BOOKS BY DR. MELISSA CAUDLE

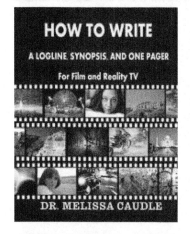

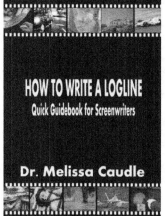

REALITY SHOW BOOKS

WWW.THEREALITYOFREALTYTV.COM

AVAILABLE ON AMAZON.COM

THE REALITY SHOW RESOURCE

www.therealitytvshowresource.com

If you want a listing on the links page, just ask for it. I'll be glad to approve a reciprocal link. While you are there, consider placing a small ad on the website to be seen thousands of times. As a reader of my book series, you get a special discount by telling me you purchased my book. Your discount code is: RT-150FILM.

HOW TO SUBMIT

A FILM OR REALITY SHOW

Many times, On the Lot Productions, LLC looks for a new film or reality show to produce. However, the company does not accept unsolicited projects. The reason is to protect me as a producer and you as a creator of a show or film. There are many reality shows and screenplays that resemble each other and we cannot be responsible for that if we already have a project similar to yours in production. To safeguard your project please register it with the WGA and/or the U.S. Library of Cons. We will not consider any screenplay or reality show concept that does not include the registration number.

To submit a project to On the Lot Productions, LLC follow these steps:

1. Email our development producer at: OTLPdevelopment@gmail.com
2. In the subject line write "Query on Film/Project – WGA # XXX)
3. Include in the body of the email the following information:

   - Registration number
   - Logline
   - Synopsis
   - Your contact information

If my development team is interested in your project, we will then send you a signed letter of confidentiality and ask you to send your business plan and script.

BOOKS IN THE SCREENWRITING GUIDEBOOK SERIES

ALL BOOKS AVAILABLE ON AMAZON.COM, BARNES & NOBLE, AND BOOKS A MILLION

NOW ACCEPTING

HEADSHOTS AND ACTOR REELS

The Keystroke Killer: Episode 1 - Transcendence

Do you want to be a part of the television Series?

Join the Facebook group to stay informed and for Casting call information etc.

THE KEYSTROKE KILLER FAN SITE

The casting directors from Los Angeles and New Orleans will use this site to scout actors. Upload your headshot and a demo reel. You may also suggest a character for a walk on role. Show us the who you want to be in a demo video. Upload a video. Let us see you!

Cast breakdown on the FILM PAGE of www.onthelotproductions.com

SUBMIT YOUR SPEC EPISODE SCRIPT TODAY!

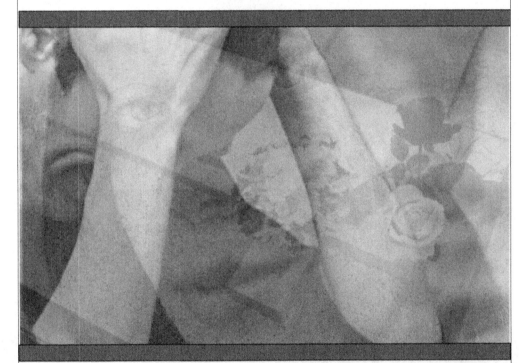

TRANSCENDENCE
Pilot Episode 1

THE KEYSTROKE KILLER

DR. MELISSA CAUDLE

HOW TO CONTACT DR. MEL

To contact Dr. Mel for a speaking engagement, training, or production help in your area, email her at drmelcaudle@gmail.com **or call 504- 264-1208.**

To purchase her books go to www.therealityofrealitytv.com **or purchase from Amazon.com.**

Dr. Mel is also available for consultation on creating your reality show, producting film or TV projects, and writing your screenplay.

www.onthelotproductions.com

650-265-1193

Printed in Great Britain
by Amazon

38414158R00119